T W I L I G H T

I N   I T A L Y

TWILIGHT

D.H. LAWRENCE

BARRIE & JENKINS
LONDON

IN ITALY

This edition first published in Great Britain in 1990 by
Barrie & Jenkins Ltd
20 Vauxhall Bridge Road, London SW1V 2SA

The publishers acknowledge the co-operation of The Estate of Frieda Lawrence Ravagli

British Library Cataloguing in Publication Data
Lawrence, D. H. (David Herbert) 1885-1930
Twilight in Italy. — (Illustrated travel series)
1. Italy. Description & travel. 1870-
I. Title   II. Series
914.5'049

ISBN 0-7126-2073-7

Designed by David Fordham
Picture research by Gabrielle Allen

Typeset by SX Composing Limited
Colour separation by Fotographics, Hong Kong
Printed and bound in Spain by Printer Industria Grafica, S.A., Barcelona

Front cover:
Lake Scene by Albert Goodwin (*Chris Beetles Gallery*)

CONTENTS

THE CRUCIFIX ACROSS
THE MOUNTAINS

T HE IMPERIAL ROAD TO ITALY GOES FROM Munich across the Tyrol, through Innsbruck and Bozen to Verona, over the mountains. Here the great processions passed as the emperors went South, or came home again from rosy Italy to their own Germany.

And how much has that old imperial vanity clung to the German soul? Did not the German kings inherit the empire of bygone Rome? It was not a very real empire, perhaps, but the sound was high and splendid.

Maybe a certain Grössenwahn is inherent in the German nature. If only nations would realise that they have certain natural characteristics, if only they could understand and agree to each other's particular nature, how much simpler it would all be.

The imperial procession no longer crosses the mountains, going South. That is almost forgotten, the road has almost passed out of mind. But still it is there, and its signs are standing.

The crucifixes are there, not mere attributes of the road, yet still having something to do with it. The imperial processions, blessed by the Pope and accompanied by the great bishops, must have planted the holy idol like a new plant among the mountains, there where it multiplied and grew according to the soil, and the race that received it.

As one goes among the Bavarian uplands and foothills, soon one realises here is another land, a strange religion. It is a strange country, remote, out of contact. Perhaps it belongs to the forgotten, imperial processions.

Coming along the clear, open roads that lead to the mountains, one scarcely notices the crucifixes and the shrines. Perhaps one's interest is dead. The crucifix itself is nothing, a factory-made piece of sentimentalism. The soul ignores it.

But gradually, one after another looming shadowily under their hoods, the crucifixes seem to create a new atmosphere over the whole countryside, a darkness, a weight in the air that is so unnaturally bright and rare with the reflection from the snows above, a darkness hovering just over the earth. So rare and unearthly the light is, from the mountains, full of strange radiance. Then every now and again recurs the crucifix, at the turning of an open, grassy road, holding a shadow and a mystery under its pointed hood.

I was startled into consciousness one evening, going alone over a marshy place at the foot of the mountains, when the sky was pale and unearthly, invisible, and the hills were nearly black. At a meeting of the tracks was a crucifix, and between the feet of the Christ were a handful of withered poppies. It was the poppies I saw, then the Christ.

It was an old shrine, the wood-sculpture of a Bavarian peasant. The Christ was a peasant of the foot of the Alps. He had broad cheekbones and sturdy limbs. His plain, rudimentary face stared fixedly at the hills, his neck was stiffened, as if in resistance to the fact of the nails and the cross, which he could not escape. It was a man nailed down in spirit, but set stubbornly against the bondage and the disgrace. He was a man of middle age, plain, crude, with some of the meanness of the peasant, but also with a kind of dogged nobility that does not yield its soul to the circumstance. Plain, almost blank in his soul, the middle-aged peasant of the crucifix resisted unmoving the misery of his position. He did not yield. His soul was set, his will was fixed. He was himself, let his circumstances be what they would, his life fixed down.

Across the marsh was a tiny square of orange-coloured light, from the farm-house with the low spreading roof. I remembered how the man and his wife and the children worked on till dark, silent and intent, carrying the hay in their arms out of the streaming thunder-rain into the shed, working silent in the soaking rain.

The body bent forward towards the earth, closing round on itself; the arms clasped full of hay, clasped round the hay that presses soft and close to the breast and the body, that pricks heat into the arms and the skin of the breast, and fills the lungs with the sleepy scent of dried herbs: the rain that falls heavily and wets the shoulders, so that the shirt clings to the hot, firm skin and the rain comes with heavy, pleasant coldness on the active flesh, running in a trickle down towards the loins, secretly; this is the peasant, this hot welter of physical sensation. And it is all intoxicating. It is intoxicating almost like a soporific, like a sensuous drug, to gather the burden to one's body in the rain, to stumble across the living

grass to the shed, to relieve one's arms of the weight, to throw down the hay on to the heap, to feel light and free in the dry shed, then to return again into the chill, hard rain, to stoop again under the rain, and rise to return again with the burden.

It is this, this endless heat and rousedness of physical sensation which keeps the body full and potent, and flushes the mind with a blood heat, a blood sleep. And this sleep, this heat of physical experience, becomes at length a bondage, at last a crucifixion. It is the life and the fulfilment of the peasant, this flow of sensuous experience. But at last it drives him almost mad, because he cannot escape.

For overhead there is always the strange radiance of the mountains, there is the mystery of the icy river rushing through its pink shoals into the darkness of the pine-woods, there is always the faint tang of ice on the air, and the rush of hoarse-sounding water.

And the ice and the upper radiance of snow are brilliant with timeless immunity from the flux and the warmth of life. Overhead they transcend all life, all the soft, moist fire of the blood. So that a man must needs live under the radiance of his own negation.

There is a strange, clear beauty of form about the men of the Bavarian highlands, about both men and women. They are large and clear and handsome in form, with blue eyes very keen, the pupil small, tightened, the iris keen, like sharp light shining on blue ice. Their large, full-moulded limbs and

erect bodies are distinct, separate, as if they were perfectly chiselled out of the stuff of life, static, cut off. Where they are everything is set back, as in a clear frosty air.

Their beauty is almost this, this strange, clean-cut isolation, as if each one of them would isolate himself still further and for ever from the rest of his fellows.

Yet they are convivial, they are almost the only race with the souls of artists. Still they act the mystery plays with instinctive fulness of interpretation, they sing strangely in the mountain fields, they love make-belief and mummery, their processions and religious festivals are profoundly impressive, solemn, and rapt.

It is a race that moves on the poles of mystic sensual delight. Every gesture is a gesture from the blood, every expression is a symbolic utterance.

For learning there is sensuous experience, for thought there is myth and drama and dancing and singing. Everything is of the blood, of the senses. There is no mind. The mind is a suffusion of physical heat, it is not separated, it is kept submerged.

At the same time, always, overhead, there is the eternal, negative radiance of the snows. Beneath is life, the hot jet of the blood playing elaborately. But above is the radiance of changeless not-being. And life passes away into this changeless radiance. Summer and the prolific blue-and-white flowering of the earth goes by, with the labour and the ecstasy of man, disappears, and is gone into brilliance that hovers overhead, the radiant cold which waits to receive back again all that which has passed for the moment into being.

The issue is too much revealed. It leaves the peasant no choice. The fate gleams transcendent above him, the brightness of eternal, unthinkable not-being. And this our life, this admixture of labour and of warm experience in the flesh, all the time it is steaming up to the changeless brilliance above, the light of the everlasting snows. This is the eternal issue.

Whether it is singing or dancing or play-acting or physical transport of love, or vengeance or cruelty, or whether it is work or sorrow or religion, the issue is always the same at last, into the radiant negation of eternity. Hence the beauty and completeness, the finality of the highland peasant. His figure, his limbs, his face, his motion, it is all formed in beauty, and it is all completed. There is no flux nor hope nor becoming, all is, once and for all. The issue is eternal, timeless, and changeless. All being and all passing away is part of the issue, which is eternal and changeless. Therefore there is no becoming and no passing away. Everything is, now and for ever. Hence the strange beauty and finality and isolation of the Bavarian peasant.

It is plain in the crucifixes. Here is the essence rendered in sculpture of wood. The face is blank and stiff, almost expressionless. One realises with a start how unchanging and conventionalised is the face of the living man and woman of these parts, handsome, but motionless as pure form. There is also an underlying meanness, secretive, cruel. It is all part of the beauty, the pure, plastic beauty. The body also of the Christus is stiff and conventionalised, yet curiously beautiful in proportion, and in the static tension which makes it unified into one clear thing. There is no movement, no possible movement. The being is fixed, finally. The whole body is locked in one knowledge, beautiful, complete. It is one with the nails. Not that it is languishing or dead. It is stubborn, knowing its own undeniable being, sure of the absolute reality of the sensuous experience. Though he is nailed down upon an irrevocable fate, yet, within that fate he has the power and the delight of all sensuous experience. So he accepts the fate and the mystic delight of the senses with one will, he is complete and final. His sensuous experience is supreme, a consummation of life and death at once.

It is the same at all times, whether it is the mowing with the scythe on the hill-slopes, or hewing the timber, or steering the raft down the river which is all effervescent with ice; whether it is drinking in the Gasthaus, or making love, or playing some mummer's part, or hating steadily and cruelly,

or whether it is kneeling in spell-bound subjection in the incense-filled church, or walking in the strange, dark, subject-procession to bless the fields, or cutting the young birch-trees for the feast of Frohenleichnam, it is always the same, the dark, powerful, mystic, sensuous experience is the whole of him, he is mindless and bound within the absoluteness of the issue, the unchangeability of the great icy not-being which holds good for ever, and is supreme.

Passing further away, towards Austria, travelling up the Isar, till the stream becomes smaller and whiter and the air is colder, the full glamour of the northern hills, which are so marvellously luminous and gleaming with flowers, wanes and gives way to a darkness, a sense of ominousness. Up there I saw another little Christ, who seemed the very soul of the place. The road went beside the river, that was seething with snowy ice-bubbles, under the rocks and the high, wolf-like pine-trees, between the pinkish shoals. The air was cold and hard and high, everything was cold and separate. And in a little glass case beside the road sat a small, hewn Christ, the head resting on the hand; and he meditates, half-wearily, doggedly, the eyebrows lifted in strange abstraction, the elbow resting on the knee. Detached, he sits and dreams and broods, wearing his little golden crown of thorns, and his little cloak of red flannel that some peasant woman has stitched for him.

No doubt he still sits there, the small, blank-faced Christ in the cloak of red flannel, dreaming, brooding, enduring,

persisting. There is a wistfulness about him, as if he knew that the whole of things was too much for him. There was no solution, either, in death. Death did not give the answer to the soul's anxiety. That which is, is. It does not cease to be when it is cut. Death cannot create nor destroy. What is, is.

The little brooding Christ knows this. What is he brooding, then? His static patience and endurance is wistful. What is it that he secretly yearns for, amid all the placidity of fate? "To be, or not to be," this may be the question, but it is not a question for death to answer. It is not a question of living or not-living. It is a question of being – to be or not to be. To persist or not to persist, that is not the question; neither is it to endure or not to endure. The issue, is it eternal not-being? If not, what, then, is being? For overhead the eternal radiance of the snow gleams unfailing, it receives the efflorescence of all life and is unchanged, the issue is bright and immortal, the snowy not-being. What, then, is being?

As one draws nearer to the turning-point of the Alps, towards the culmination and the southern slope, the influence of the educated world is felt once more. Bavaria is remote in spirit, as yet unattached. Its crucifixes are old and grey and abstract, small like the kernel of the truth. Further into Austria they become new, they are painted white, they are larger, more obtrusive. They are the expressions of a later, newer phase, more introspective and self-conscious. But still they are genuine expressions of the people's soul.

Often, one can distinguish the work of a particular artist here and there in a district. In the Zemm valley, in the heart of the Tyrol, behind Innsbruck, there are five or six crucifixes by one sculptor. He is no longer a peasant working out an idea, conveying a dogma. He is an artist, trained and conscious, probably working in Vienna. He is consciously trying to convey a *feeling*, he is no longer striving awkwardly to render a truth, a religious fact.

The chief of his crucifixes stands deep in the Klamm, in the dank gorge where it is always half-night. The road runs under the rock and the trees, half-way up the one side of the pass. Below, the stream rushes ceaselessly, embroiled among great stones, making an endless loud noise. The rock face opposite rises high overhead, with the sky far up. So that one is walking in a half-night, an underworld. And just below the path, where the pack-horses go climbing to the remote, infolded villages, in the cold gloom of the pass hangs the large, pale Christ. He is larger than life-size. He has fallen forward, just dead, and the weight of the full-grown, mature body hangs on the nails of the hands. So the dead, heavy body drops forward, sags, as if it would tear away and fall under its own weight.

It is the end. The face is barren with a dead expression of weariness, and brutalised with pain and bitterness. The rather ugly, passionate mouth is set for ever in the disillusionment of death. Death is the complete disillusionment, set like a seal over the whole body and being, over the suffering and weariness and the bodily passion.

The pass is gloomy and damp, the water roars unceasingly, till it is almost like a constant pain. The driver of the pack-horses, as he comes up the narrow path in the side of the gorge, cringes his sturdy cheerfulness as if to obliterate himself, drawing near to the large, pale Christ, and he takes his hat off as he passes, though he does not look up, but keeps his face averted from the crucifix. He hurries by in the gloom, climbing the steep path after his horses, and the large white Christ hangs extended above.

The driver of the pack-horses is afraid. The fear is always there in him, in spite of his sturdy, healthy robustness. His soul is not sturdy. It is blenched and whitened with fear. The mountains are dark overhead, the water roars in the gloom below. His heart is ground between the mill-stones of dread. When he passes the extended body of the dead Christ he takes off his hat to the Lord of Death. Christ is the Deathly One, He is Death incarnate.

And the driver of the pack-horses acknowledges this deathly Christ as supreme Lord. The mountain peasant seems grounded upon fear, the fear of death, of physical death. Beyond this he knows nothing. His supreme sensation is in physical pain, and in its culmination. His great climax, his consummation, is death. Therefore he worships it, bows down before it, and is fascinated by it all the while. It is his fulfilment, death, and his approach to fulfilment is through physical pain.

And so these monuments to physical death are found everywhere in the valleys. By the same hand that carved the big Christ, a little further on, at the end of a bridge, was another crucifix, a small one. This Christ had a fair beard, and was thin, and his body was hanging almost lightly, whereas the other Christ was large and dark and handsome. But in this, as well as in the other, was the same neutral triumph of death, complete, negative death, so complete as to be abstract, beyond cynicism in its completeness of leaving off.

Everywhere is the same obsession with the fact of physical

pain, accident, and sudden death. Wherever a misfortune has befallen a man, there is nailed up a little memorial of the event, in propitiation of the God of hurt and death. A man is standing up to his waist in water, drowning in full stream, his arms in the air. The little painting in its wooden frame is nailed to the tree, the spot is sacred to the accident. Again, another little crude picture fastened to a rock: a tree, falling on a man's leg, smashes it like a stalk, while the blood flies up. Always there is the strange ejaculation of anguish and fear, perpetuated in the little paintings nailed up in the place of the disaster.

This is the worship, then, the worship of death and the approaches to death, physical violence, and pain. There is something crude and sinister about it, almost like depravity, a form of reverting, turning back along the course of blood by which we have come.

Turning the ridge on the great road to the south, the imperial road to Rome, a decisive change takes place. The Christs have been taking on various different characters, all of them more or less realistically conveyed. One Christus is very elegant, combed and brushed and foppish on his cross, as Gabriele D'Annunzio's son posing as a martyred saint. The martyrdom of this Christ is according to the most polite convention. The elegance is very important, and very Austrian. One might almost imagine the young man had taken up this striking and original position to create a delightful sensation among the ladies. It is quite in the Viennese spirit. There is something brave and keen in it, too. The individual pride of body triumphs over every difficulty in the situation. The pride and satisfaction in the clean, elegant form, the perfectly trimmed hair, the exquisite bearing, are more important than the fact of death or pain. This may be foolish, it is at the same time admirable.

But the tendency of the crucifix, as it nears the ridge to the south, is to become weak and sentimental. The carved Christs turn up their faces and roll back their eyes very piteously, in the approved Guido Reni fashion. They are overdoing the pathetic turn. They are looking to heaven and thinking about themselves in self-commiseration. Others again are beautiful as elegies. It is dead Hyacinth lifted and extended to view, in all his beautiful, dead youth. The young, male body droops forward on the cross, like a dead flower. It looks as if its only true nature were to be dead. How lovely is death, how poignant, real, and satisfying! It is the true elegiac spirit.

Then there are the ordinary, factory-made Christs, which are not very significant. There are as null as the Christs we see represented in England, just vulgar nothingness. But these figures have gashes of red, a red paint of blood, which is sensational.

Beyond the Brenner, I have only seen vulgar or sensational crucifixes. There are great gashes on the breast and the knees of the Christ-figure, and the scarlet flows out and trickles down, till the crucified body has become a ghastly striped

thing of red and white, just a sickly thing of striped red.

They paint the rocks at the corners of the tracks, among the mountains; a blue and white ring for the road to Ginzling, a red smear for the way to St. Jakob. So one follows the blue and white ring, or the three stripes of blue and white, or the red smear, as the case may be. And the red on the rocks, the dabs of red paint, are of just the same colour as the red upon the crucifixes; so that the red upon the crucifixes is paint, and the signs on the rocks are sensational, like blood.

I remember the little brooding Christ of the Isar, in his little cloak of red flannel and his crown of gilded thorns, and he remains real and dear to me, among all this violence of representation.

"Couvre-toi de gloire, Tartarin – couvre-toi de flanelle." Why should it please me so that his cloak is of red flannel?

In a valley near St. Jakob, just over the ridge, a long way from the railway, there is a very big, important shrine by the roadside. It is a chapel built in the baroque manner, florid pink and cream outside, with opulent small arches. And inside is the most startlingly sensational Christus I have ever seen. He is a big, powerful man, seated after the crucifixion, perhaps after the resurrection, sitting by the grave. He sits sideways, as if the extremity were over, finished, the agitation done with, only the result of the experience remaining. There is some blood on his powerful, naked, defeated body, that sits rather hulked. But it is the face which is so terrifying. It is slightly turned over the hulked, crucified shoulder, to look. And the look of this face, of which the body has been killed, is beyond all expectation horrible. The eyes look at one, yet have no seeing in them, they seem to see only their own blood. For they are bloodshot till the whites are scarlet, the iris is purpled. These red, bloody eyes with their stained pupils, glancing awfully at all who enter the shrine, looking as if to see through the blood of the late brutal death, are terrible. The naked, strong body has known death, and sits in utter dejection, finished, hulked, a weight of shame. And what remains of life is in the face, whose expression is sinister and gruesome, like that of an unrelenting criminal violated by torture. The criminal look of misery and hatred on the fixed, violated face and in the bloodshot eyes is almost impossible. He is conquered, beaten, broken, his body is a mass of torture, an unthinkable shame. Yet his will remains obstinate and ugly, integral with utter hatred.

It is a great shock to find this figure sitting in a handsome, baroque, pink-washed shrine in one of those Alpine valleys which to our thinking are all flowers and romance, like the picture in the Tate Gallery. "Spring in the Austrian Tyrol" is to our minds a vision of pristine loveliness. It contains also this

Christ of the heavy body defiled by torture and death, the strong, virile life overcome by physical violence, the eyes still looking back bloodshot in consummate hate and misery.

The shrine was well kept and evidently much used. It was hung with ex-voto limbs and with many gifts. It was a centre of worship, of a sort of almost obscene worship. Afterwards the black pine-trees and the river of that valley seemed unclean, as if an unclean spirit lived there. The very flowers seemed unnatural, and the white gleam on the mountain-tops was a glisten of supreme, cynical horror.

After this, in the populous valleys, all the crucifixes were more or less tainted and vulgar. Only high up, where the crucifix becomes smaller and smaller, is there left any of the old beauty and religion. Higher and higher, the monument becomes smaller and smaller, till in the snows it stands out like a post, or a thick arrow stuck barb upwards. The crucifix itself is a small thing under the pointed hood, the barb of the arrow. The snow blows under the tiny shed, upon the little, exposed Christ. All round is the solid whiteness of snow, the awful curves and concaves of pure whiteness of the montain top, the hollow whiteness between the peaks, where the path crosses the high, extreme ridge of the pass. And here stands the last crucifix, half buried, small and tufted with snow. The guides tramp slowly, heavily past, not observing the presence of the symbol, making no salute. Further down, every mountain peasant lifted his hat. But the guide tramps by without concern. His is a professional importance now.

On a small mountain track on the Jaufen, not far from Meran, was a fallen Christus. I was hurrying downhill to escape from an icy wind which almost took away my consciousness, and I was looking up at the gleaming, unchanging snow-peaks all round. They seemed like blades immortal in the sky. So I almost ran into a very old Martertafel. It leaned on the cold, stony hillside, surrounded by the white peaks in the upper air.

The wooden hood was silver-grey with age, and covered, on the top, with a thicket of lichen, which stuck up in hoary tufts. But on the rock at the foot of the post was the fallen Christ, armless, who had tumbled down and lay in an unnatural posture, the naked, ancient wooden sculpture of the body on the naked, living rock. It was one of the old uncouth Christs hewn out of bare wood, having the long, wedge-shaped limbs and thin flat legs that are significant of the true spirit, the desire to convey a religious truth, not a sensational experience.

The arms of the fallen Christ had broken off at the shoulders, and they hung on their nails, as ex-voto limbs hang in the shrines. But these arms dangled from the palms, one at each end of the cross, the muscles, carved sparely in the old wood, looking all wrong, upside down. And the icy wind blew them backwards and forwards, so that they gave a painful impression, there in the stark, sterile place of rock and cold. Yet I dared not touch the fallen body of the Christ, that lay on its back in so grotesque a posture at the foot of the post. I wondered who would come and take the broken thing away, and for what purpose.

The Monastery.

ON THE
LAGO DI GARDA

THE SPINNER AND
THE MONKS

T HE HOLY SPIRIT IS A DOVE, OR AN EAGLE. IN THE Old Testament it was an Eagle; in the New Testament it is a Dove.

And there are, standing over the Christian world, the Churches of the Dove and the Churches of the Eagle. There are, moreover, the Churches which do not belong to the Holy Spirit at all, but which are built to pure fancy and logic; such as the Wren Churches in London.

The Churches of the Dove are shy and hidden; they nestle among trees, and their bells sound in the mellowness of Sunday; or they are gathered into a silence of their own in the very midst of the town, so that one passes them by without observing them; they are as if invisible, offering no resistance to the storming of the traffic.

But the Churches of the Eagle stand high, with their heads to the skies, as if they challenged the world below. They are the Churches of the Spirit of David, and their bells ring passionately, imperiously, falling on the subservient world below.

The Church of San Francesco was a Church of the Dove. I passed it several times, in the dark, silent little square, without knowing it was a church. Its pink walls were blind, windowless, unnoticeable, it gave no sign, unless one caught sight of the tan curtain hanging in the door, and the slit of darkness beneath. Yet it was the chief church of the village.

But the Church of San Tommaso perched over the village. Coming down the cobbled, submerged street, many a time I looked up between the houses and saw the thin old church standing above in the light, as if it perched on the house-roofs. Its thin grey neck was held up stiffly, beyond was a vision of dark foliage, and the high hillside.

I saw it often, and yet for a long time it never occurred to me that it actually existed. It was like a vision, a thing one does not expect to come close to. It was there standing away upon the house-tops, against a glamour of foliaged hillside. I was submerged in the village, on the uneven, cobbled street, between old high walls and cavernous shops and the houses with flights of steps.

For a long time I knew how the day went, by the imperious clangour of mid-day and evening bells striking down upon the houses and the edge of the lake. Yet it did not occur to me to ask where these bells rang. Till at last my everyday trance was broken in upon, and I knew the ringing of the Church of San Tommaso. The church became a living connection with me.

So I set out to find it, I wanted to go to it. It was very near. I could see it from the piazza by the lake. And the village itself had only a few hundreds of inhabitants. The church must be within a stone's-throw.

Yet I could not find it. I went out of the back door of the house, into the narrow gully of the back street. Women glanced down at me from the top of the flights of steps, old

men stood, half-turning, half-crouching under the dark shadow of the walls, to stare. It was as if the strange creatures of the under-shadow were looking at me. I was of another element.

The Italian people are called "Children of the Sun". They might better be called "Children of the Shadow". Their souls are dark and nocturnal. If they are to be easy, they must be able to hide, to be hidden in lairs and caves of darkness. Going through these tiny chaotic back-ways of the village was like venturing through the labyrinth made by furtive creatures, who watched from out of another element. And I was pale, and clear, and evanescent, like the light, and they were dark, and close, and constant, like the shadow.

So I was quite baffled by the tortuous, tiny, deep passages of the village. I could not find my way. I hurried towards the broken end of a street, where the sunshine and the olive trees looked like a mirage before me. And there above me I saw the thin, stiff neck of old San Tommaso, grey and pale in the sun. Yet I could not get up to the church, I found myself again on the piazza.

Another day, however, I found a broken staircase, where weeds grew in the gaps the steps had made in falling, and maidenhair hung on the darker side of the wall. I went up un-willingly, because the Italians used this old staircase as a privy, as they will any deep side-passage.

But I ran up the broken stairway, and came out suddenly, as by a miracle, clean on the platform of my San Tommaso, in the tremendous sunshine.

It was another world, the world of the eagle, the world of fierce abstraction. It was all clear, overwhelming sunshine, a platform hung in the light. Just below were the confused, tiled roofs of the village, and beyond them the pale blue water, down below; and opposite, opposite my face and breast, the clear, luminous snow of the mountain across the lake, level with me apparently, though really much above.

I was in the skies now, looking down from my square terrace of cobbled pavement, that was worn like the threshold of the ancient church. Round the terrace ran a low, broad wall, the coping of the upper heaven where I had climbed.

There was a blood-red sail like a butterfly breathing down on the blue water, whilst the earth on the near side gave off a green-silver smoke of olive trees, coming up and around the earth-coloured roofs.

It always remains to me that San Tommaso and its terrace hang suspended above the village, like the lowest step of heaven, of Jacob's ladder. Behind, the land rises in a high sweep. But the terrace of San Tommaso is let down from heaven, and does not touch the earth.

I went into the church. It was very dark, and impregnated with centuries of incense. It affected me like the lair of some enormous creature. My senses were roused, they sprang awake in the hot, spiced darkness. My skin was expectant, as if it expected some contact, some embrace, as if it were aware of the contiguity of the physical world, the physical contact with the darkness and the heavy, suggestive substance of the enclosure. It was a thick, fierce darkness of the senses. But my soul shrank.

I went out again. The pavemented threshold was clear as a jewel, the marvellous clarity of sunshine that becomes blue in the height seemed to distil me into itself.

Across, the heavy mountain crouched along the side of the lake, the upper half brilliantly white, belonging to the sky, the lower half dark and grim. So, then, that is where heaven and earth are divided. From behind me, on the left, the headland swept down out of a great, pale-grey, arid height, through a rush of russet and crimson, to the olive smoke and the water of the level earth. And between, like the blade of the sky cleaving the earth asunder, went the pale-blue lake, cleaving mountain from mountain with the triumph of the sky.

Then I noticed that a big, blue-checked cloth was spread on the parapet before me, over the parapet of heaven. I wondered why it hung there.

Turning round, on the other side of the terrace, under a caper-bush that hung like a blood-stain from the grey wall above her, stood a little grey woman whose fingers were busy. Like the grey church, she made me feel as if I were not in existence. I was wandering by the parapet of heaven, looking down. But she stood back against the solid wall, under the caper-bush, unobserved and unobserving. She was like a fragment of earth, she was a living stone of the terrace, sun-bleached. She took no notice of me, who was hesitating looking down at the earth beneath. She stood back under the sun-bleached solid wall, like a stone rolled down and stayed in a crevice.

Her head was tied in a dark-red kerchief, but pieces of hair, like dirty snow, quite short, stuck out over her ears. And she was spinning. I wondered so much, that I could not cross towards her. She was grey, and her apron, and her dress, and her kerchief, and her hands and her face were all sun-bleached and sun-stained, greyey, bluey, browny, like stones and half-coloured leaves, sunny in their colourlessness. In my black coat, I felt myself wrong, false, an outsider.

She was spinning, spontaneously, like a little wind. Under her arm she held a distaff of dark, ripe wood, just a straight stick with a clutch at the end, like a grasp of brown fingers full of a fluff of blackish, rusty fleece, held up near her shoulder. And her fingers were plucking spontaneously at the strands of wool drawn down from it. And hanging near her feet, spinning round upon a black thread, spinning busily, like a thing in a gay wind, was her shuttle, her bobbin wound fat with the coarse, blackish worsted she was making.

All the time, like motion without thought, her fingers teased out the fleece, drawing it down to a fairly uniform thickness: brown, old, natural fingers that worked as in a sleep, the thumb having a long grey nail; and from moment to moment there was a quick, downward rub, between thumb and forefinger, of the thread that hung in front of her apron, the heavy bobbin spun more briskly, and she felt again at the fleece as she drew it down, and she gave a twist to the thread that issued, and the bobbin spun swiftly.

Her eyes were clear as the sky, blue, empyrean, transcendent. They were clear, but they had no looking in them. Her face was like a sun-worn stone.

"You are spinning," I said to her.

Her eyes glanced over me, making no effort of attention.

"Yes," she said.

She saw merely a man's figure, a stranger, standing near. I was a bit of the outside, negligible. She remained as she was, clear and sustained like an old stone upon the hillside. She stood short and sturdy, looking for the most part straight in front, unseeing, but glancing from time to time, with a little, unconscious attention, at the thread. She was slightly more animated than the sunshine and the stone and the motionless caper-bush above her. Still her fingers went along the strand of fleece near her breast.

"That is an old way of spinning," I said.

"What?"

She looked up at me with eyes clear and transcendent as the heavens. But she was slightly roused. There was the slight motion of the eagle in her turning to look at me, a faint gleam of rapt light in her eyes. It was my unaccustomed Italian.

"That is an old way of spinning," I repeated.

"Yes – an old way," she repeated, as if to say the words so that they should be natural to her. And I became to her merely a transient circumstance, a man, part of the surroundings. We divided the gift of speech, that was all.

She glanced at me again, with her wonderful, unchanging eyes, that were like the visible heavens, unthinking, or like two flowers that are open in pure clear unconsciousness. To her I was a piece of the environment. That was all. Her world was clear and absolute, without consciousness of self. She was not self-conscious, because she was not aware that there was anything in the universe except *her* universe. In her universe I was a stranger, a foreign *signore*. That I had a world of my own, other than her own, was not conceived by her. She did not care.

So we conceive the stars. We are told that they are other worlds. But the stars are the clustered and single gleaming lights in the night-sky of our world. When I come home at night, there are the stars. When I cease to exist as the microcosm, when I begin to think of the cosmos, then the stars are other worlds. Then the macrocosm absorbs me. But the

macrocosm is not me. It is something which I, the micro-cosm, am not.

So that there is something which is unknown to me and which nevertheless exists. I am finite, and my understanding has limits. The universe is bigger than I shall ever see, in mind or spirit. There is that which is not me.

If I say "The plant Mars is inhabited," I do not know what I mean by "inhabited," with reference to the planet Mars. I can only mean that that world is not my world. I can only know there is that which is not me. I am the microcosm, but the macrocosm is that also which I am not.

The old woman on the terrace in the sun did not know this. She was herself the core and centre to the world, the sun, and the single firmament. She knew that I was an in-habitant of lands which she had never seen. But what of that! There were parts of her own body which she had never seen, which physiologically she could never see. They were none the less her own because she had never seen them. The lands she had not seen were corporate parts of her own living body, the knowledge she had not attained was only the hid-den knowledge of her own self. She *was* the substance of the knowledge, whether she had the knowledge in her mind or not. There was nothing which was not herself, ultimately. Even the man, the male, was part of herself. He was the mobile, separate part, but he was none the less herself because he was sometimes severed from her. If every apple in the world were cut in two, the apple would not be changed. The reality is the apple, which is just the same in the half-apple as in the whole.

And she, the old spinning-woman, was the apple, eternal, unchangeable, whole even in her partiality. It was this which gave the wonderful clear unconsciousness to her eyes. How could she be conscious of herself when all was herself?

She was talking to me of a sheep that had died, but I could not understand because of her dialect. It never occurred to her that I could not understand. She only thought me dif-ferent, stupid. And she talked on. The ewes had lived under the house, and a part was divided off for the he-goat, because the other people brought their she-goats to be covered by the he-goat. But how the ewe came to die I could not make out.

Her fingers worked away all the time in a little, half-fretful movement, yet spontaneous as butterflies leaping here and there. She chattered rapidly on in her Italian that I could not understand, looking meanwhile into my face, because the story roused her somewhat. Yet not a feature moved. Her eyes remained candid and open and unconscious as the skies. Only a sharp will in them now and then seemed to gleam at me, as if to dominate me.

Her shuttle had caught in a dead chicory plant, and spun no more. She did not notice. I stooped and broke off the twigs. There was a glint of blue on them yet. Seeing what I was doing, she merely withdrew a few inches from the plant. Her bobbin hung free.

She went on with her tale, looking at me wonderfully. She

seemed like the Creation, like the beginning of the world, the first morning. Her eyes were like the first morning of the world, so ageless.

Her thread broke. She seemed to take no notice, but mechanically picked up the shuttle, wound up a length of worsted, connected the ends from her wool strand, set the bobbin spinning again, and went on talking, in her half-intimate, half-unconscious fashion, as if she were talking to her own world in me.

So she stood in the sunshine on the little platform, old and yet like the morning, erect and solitary, sun-coloured, sun-discoloured, whilst I at her elbow, like a piece of night and moonshine, stood smiling into her eyes, afraid lest she should deny me existence.

Which she did. She had stopped talking, did not look at me any more, but went on with her spinning, the brown shuttle twisting gaily. So she stood, belonging to the sunshine and the weather, taking no more notice of me than of the dark-stained caper-bush which hung from the wall above her head, whilst I, waiting at her side, was like the moon in the daytime sky, overshone, obliterated, in spite of my black clothes.

"How long has it taken you to do that much?" I asked.

She waited a minute, glanced at her bobbin.

"This much? I don't know. A day or two."

"But you do it quickly."

She looked at me, as if suspiciously and derisively. Then, quite suddenly, she started forward and went across the terrace to the great blue-and-white checked cloth that was drying on the wall. I hesitated. She had cut off her consciousness from me. So I turned and ran away, taking the steps two at a time, to get away from her. In a moment I was between the walls, climbing upwards, hidden.

The school-mistress had told me I should find snowdrops behind San Tommaso. If she had not asserted such confident knowledge I should have doubted her translation of *perce-neige*. She meant Christmas roses all the while.

However, I went looking for snowdrops. The walls broke down suddenly, and I was out in a grassy olive orchard, following a track beside pieces of fallen overgrown masonry. So I came to skirt the brink of a steep little gorge, at the bottom of which a stream was rushing down its steep slant to the lake. Here I stood to look for my snowdrops. The grassy, rocky bank went down steep from my feet. I heard water tittle-tattling away in deep shadow below. There were pale flecks in the dimness, but these, I knew, were primroses. So I scrambled down.

Looking up, out of the heavy shadow that lay in the cleft, I could see, right in the sky, grey rocks shining transcendent in the pure empyrean. "Are they so far up?" I thought. I did not dare to say, "Am I so far down?" But I was uneasy. Nevertheless it was a lovely place, in the cold shadow, complete; when one forgot the shining rocks far above, it was a complete, shadowless world of shadow. Primroses were everywhere in

nests of pale bloom upon the dark, steep face of the cleft, and tongues of fern hanging out, and here and there under the rods and twigs of bushes were tufts of wrecked Christmas roses, nearly over, but still, in the coldest corners, the lovely buds like handfuls of snow. There had been such crowded sumptuous tufts of Christmas roses everywhere in the stream-gullies, during the shadow of winter, that these few remaining flowers were hardly noticeable.

I gathered instead the primroses, that smelled of earth and of the weather. There were no snowdrops. I had found the day before a bank of crocuses, pale, fragile, lilac-coloured flowers with dark veins, pricking up keenly like myriad little lilac-coloured flames among the grass, under the olive trees. And I wanted very much to find the snowdrops hanging in the gloom. But there were not any.

I gathered a handful of primroses, then I climbed suddenly, quickly out of the deep watercourse, anxious to get back to the sunshine before the evening fell. Up above I saw

the olive trees in their sunny golden grass, and sunlit grey rocks immensely high up. I was afraid lest the evening would fall whilst I was groping about like an otter in the damp and the darkness, that the day of sunshine would be over.

Soon I was up in the sunshine again, on the turf under the olive trees, reassured. It was the upper world of glowing light, and I was safe again.

All the olives were gathered, and the mills were going night and day, making a great, acrid scent of olive oil in preparation, by the lake. The little stream rattled down. A mule driver "Hued!" to his mules on the Strada Vecchia. High up, on the Strada Nuova, the beautiful, new, military high-road, which winds with beautiful curves up the mountain-side, crossing the same stream several times in clear-leaping bridges, travelling cut out of sheer slope high above the lake, winding beautifully and gracefully forward to the Austrian frontier, where it ends: high up on the lovely swinging road, in the strong evening sunshine, I saw a bullock wagon

moving like a vision, though the clanking of the wagon and the crack of the bullock whip resounded close in my ears.

Everything was clear and sun-coloured up there, clear-grey rocks partaking of the sky, tawny grass and scrub, browny-green spires of cypresses, and then the mist of grey-green olives fuming down to the lake-side. There was no shadow, only clear sun-substance built up to the sky, a bullock wagon moving slowly in the high sunlight, along the uppermost terrace of the military road. I sat in the warm stillness of the transcendent afternoon.

The four o'clock steamer was creeping down the lake from the Austrian end, creeping under the cliffs. Far away, the Verona side, beyond the Island, lay fused in dim gold. The mountain opposite was so still, that my heart seemed to fade in its beating, as if it too would be still. All was perfectly still, pure substance. The little steamer on the floor of the world below, the mules down the road cast no shadow. They

too were pure sun-substance travelling on the surface of the sun-made world.

A cricket hopped near me. Then I remembered that it was Saturday afternoon, when a strange suspension comes over the world. And then, just below me, I saw two monks walking in their garden between the naked, bony vines, walking in their wintry garden of bony vines and olive trees, their brown cassocks passing between the brown vine-stocks, their heads bare to the sunshine, sometimes a glint of light as their feet strode from under their skirts.

It was so still, everything so perfectly suspended, that I felt them talking. They marched with the peculiar march of monks, a long, loping stride, their heads together, their skirts swaying slowly, two brown monks with hidden hands, sliding under the bony vines and beside the cabbages, their heads always together in hidden converse. It was as if I were attending with my dark soul to their inaudible undertone. All the time I sat still in silence, I was one with them, a partaker, though I could hear no sound of their voices. I went with the long stride of their skirted feet, that slid springless and noiseless from end to end of the garden, and back again. Their hands were kept down at their sides, hidden in the long sleeves and the skirts of their robes. They did not touch each other, nor gesticulate as they walked. There was no motion save the long, furtive stride and the heads leaning together. Yet there was an eagerness in their conversation. Almost like shadow-creatures ventured out of their cold, obscure element, they went backwards and forwards in their wintry garden, thinking nobody could see them.

Across, above them, was the faint, rousing dazzle of snow. They never looked up. But the dazzle of snow began to glow as they walked, the wonderful, faint, ethereal flush of the long range of snow in the heavens, at evening, began to kindle. Another world was coming to pass, the cold, rare night. It was dawning in exquisite, icy rose upon the long mountain-summit opposite. The monks walked backwards and forwards, talking, in the first undershadow.

And I noticed that up above the snow, frail in the bluish sky, a frail moon had put forth, like a thin, scalloped film of ice floated out on the slow current of the coming night. And a bell sounded.

And still the monks were pacing backwards and forwards, backwards and forwards, with a strange, neutral regularity.

The shadows were coming across everything, because of the mountains in the west. Already the olive wood where I sat was extinguished. This was the world of the monks, the rim of pallor between night and day. Here they paced, backwards and forwards, backwards and forwards, in the neutral, shadowless light of shadow.

Neither the flare of day nor the completeness of night reached them, they paced the narrow path of the twilight, treading in the neutrality of the law. Neither the blood nor the spirit spoke in them, only the law, the abstraction of the average. The infinite is positive and negative. But the average is only neutral. And the monks trod backward and forward down the line of neutrality.

Meanwhile, on the length of mountain-ridge, the snow grew rosy-incandescent, like heaven breaking into blossom. After all, eternal not-being and eternal being are the same. In the rosy snow that shone in heaven over a darkened earth was the ecstasy of consummation. Night and day are one, light and dark are one, both the same in the origin and in the issue, both the same in the moment of ecstasy, light fused in darkness and darkness fused in light, as in the rosy snow above the twilight.

But in the monks it was not ecstasy, in them it was neutrality, the under earth. Transcendent, above the shadowed, twilit earth was the rosy snow of ecstasy. But spreading far over us, down below, was the neutrality of the twilight, of the monks. The flesh neutralising the spirit, the spirit neutralising the flesh, the law of the average asserted, this was the monks as they paced backward and forward.

The moon climbed higher, away from the snowy, fading ridge, she became gradually herself. Between the roots of the olive tree was a rosy-tipped daisy just going to sleep. I gathered it and put it among the frail, moony little bunch of primroses, so that its sleep should warm the rest. Also I put in some little periwinkles, that were very blue, reminding me of the eyes of the old woman.

The day was gone, the twilight was gone, and the snow was invisible as I came down to the side of the lake. Only the moon, white and shining, was in the sky, like a woman glorying in her own loveliness as she loiters superbly to the gaze of all the world, looking sometimes through the fringe of dark olive leaves, sometimes looking at her own superb, quivering body, wholly naked in the water of the lake.

My little old woman was gone. She, all day-sunshine, would have none of the moon. Always she must live like a bird, looking down on all the world at once, so that it lay all subsidiary to herself, herself the wakeful consciousness hovering over the world like a hawk, like a sleep of wakefulness. And, like a bird, she went to sleep as the shadows came.

She did not know the yielding up of the senses and the possession of the unknown, through the senses, which happens under a superb moon. The all-glorious sun knows none of these yieldings up. He takes his way. And the daisies at once go to sleep. And the soul of the old spinning-woman also closed up at sunset, the rest was a sleep, a cessation.

It is all so strange and varied: the dark-skinned Italians ecstatic in the night and the moon, the blue-eyed old woman ecstatic in the busy sunshine, the monks in the garden below, who are supposed to unite both, passing only in the neutrality of the average. Where, then, is the meeting-point: where in mankind is the ecstasy of light and dark together, the supreme transcendence of the afterglow, day hovering in the embrace of the coming night like two angels embracing in the heavens, like Eurydice in the arms of Orpheus, or Persephone embraced by Pluto?

Where is the supreme ecstasy in mankind, which makes day a delight and night a delight, purpose an ecstasy and a concourse in ecstasy, and single abandon of the single body and soul also an ecstasy under the moon? Where is the transcendent knowledge in our hearts, uniting sun and darkness, day and night, spirit and senses? Why do we not know that the two in consummation are one; that each is only part; partial and alone for ever; but that the two in consummation are perfect, beyond the range of loneliness or solitude?

ON THE
LAGO DI GARDA
THE LEMON
GARDENS

T HE PADRONE CAME JUST AS WE WERE DRINKING coffee after dinner. It was two o'clock, because the steamer going down the lake to Desenzano had bustled through the sunshine, and the rocking of the water still made lights that danced up and down upon the wall among the shadows by the piano.

The signore was very apologetic. I found him bowing in the hall, cap in one hand, a slip of paper in the other, protesting eagerly, in broken French, against disturbing me.

He is a little, shrivelled man, with close-cropped grey hair on his skull, and a protruding jaw, which, with his gesticulations, always makes me think of an ancient, aristocratic monkey. The signore is a gentleman, and the last, shrivelled representative of his race. His only outstanding quality, according to the villagers, is his avarice.

"Mais – mais, monsieur – je crains que – que – que je vous dérange – "

He spreads wide his hands and bows, looking up at me with implicit brown eyes, so ageless in his wrinkled, monkey's face, like onyx. He loves to speak French, because then he feels grand. He has a queer, naïve, ancient passion to be grand. As the remains of an impoverished family, he is not much better than a well-to-do peasant. But the old spirit is eager and pathetic in him.

He loves to speak French to me. He holds his chin and waits, in his anxiety for the phrase to come. Then it stammers

forth, a little rush, ending in Italian. But his pride is all on edge: we must continue in French.

The hall is cold, yet he will not come into the large room. This is not a courtesy visit. He is not here in his quality of gentleman. He is only an anxious villager.

"Voyez, monsieur – cet – cet – qu'est-ce que – qu'est-ce que veut dire cet – cela?"

He shows me the paper. It is an old scrap of print, the picture of an American patent door-spring, with directions: "Fasten the spring either end up. Wind it up. Never unwind."

It is laconic and American. The signore watches me anxiously, waiting, holding his chin. He is afraid he ought to understand my English. I stutter off into French, confounded by the laconic phrases of the directions. Nevertheless, I make it clear what the paper says.

He cannot believe me. It must say something else as well. He has not done anything contrary to these directions. He is most distressed.

"Mais, monsieur, la porte – la porte – elle ferme *pas* – elle s'ouvre – "

He skipped to the door and showed me the whole tragic mystery. The door, it is shut – ecco! He releases the catch, and pouf! – she flies open. She flies *open*. It is quite final.

The brown, expressionless, ageless eyes, that remind me of a monkey's, or of onyx, wait for me. I feel the responsibility devolve upon me. I am anxious.

"Allow me," I said, "to come and look at the door."

I feel uncomfortably like Sherlock Holmes. The padrone protests – non, monsieur, non, cela vous dérange – that he only wanted me to translate the words, he does not want to disturb me. Nevertheless, we go. I feel I have the honour of mechanical England in my hands.

The Casa di Paoli is quite a splendid place. It is large, pink and cream, rising up to a square tower in the centre, throwing off a painted loggia at either extreme of the façade. It stands a little way back from the road, just above the lake, and grass grows on the bay of cobbled pavement in front. When at night the moon shines full on this pale façade, the theatre is far outdone in staginess.

The hall is spacious and beautiful, with great glass doors at either end, through which shine the courtyards where bamboos fray the sunlight and geraniums glare red. The floor is of soft red tiles, oiled and polished like glass, the walls are washed grey-white, the ceiling is painted with pink roses and birds. This is half-way between the outer world and the interior world, it partakes of both.

The other rooms are dark and ugly. There is no mistake about their being interior. They are like furnished vaults. The red-tiled, polished floor in the drawing-room seems cold and clammy, the carved, cold furniture stands in its tomb, the air has been darkened and starved to death, it is perished.

Outside, the sunshine runs like birds singing. Up above, the grey rocks build the sun-substance in heaven, San Tommaso guards the terrace. But inside here is the immemorial shadow.

Again I had to think of the Italian soul, how it is dark, cleaving to the eternal night. It seems to have become so, at the Renaissance, after the Renaissance.

In the Middle Ages Christian Europe seems to have been striving, out of a strong, primitive, animal nature, towards the self-abnegation and the abstraction of Christ. This brought about by itself a great sense of completeness. The two halves were joined by the effort towards the one as yet unrealised. There was a triumphant joy in the Whole.

But the movement all the time was in one direction,

towards the elimination of the flesh. Man wanted more and more to become purely free and abstract. Pure freedom was in pure abstraction. The Word was absolute. When man became as the Word, a pure law, then he was free.

But when this conclusion was reached, the movement broke. Already Botticelli painted Aphrodite, queen of the senses, supreme along with Mary, Queen of Heaven. And Michael Angelo suddenly turned back on the whole Christian movement, back to the flesh. The flesh was supreme and god-like, in the oneness of the flesh, in the oneness of our physical being, we are one with God, with the Father. God the Father created man in the flesh, in His own image. Michael Angelo swung right back to the old Mosaic position. Christ did not exist. To Michael Angelo there was no salvation in the spirit. There was God the Father, the Begetter, the Author of all flesh. And there was the inexorable law of the flesh, the Last Judgement, the fall of the immortal flesh into Hell.

This has been the Italian position ever since. The mind, that is the Light; the senses, they are the Darkness. Aphrodite, the queen of the senses, she, born of the sea-foam, is the luminousness of the gleaming senses, the phosphorescence of the sea, the senses become a conscious aim unto themselves; she is the gleaming darkness, she is the luminous night, she is goddess of destruction, her white, cold fire consumes and does not create.

This is the soul of the Italian since the Renaissance. In the sunshine he basks asleep, gathering up a vintage into his veins which in the night-time he will distil into ecstatic sensual delight, the intense, white-cold ecstasy of darkness and moonlight, the raucous, cat-like, destructive enjoyment, the senses conscious and crying out in their consciousness in the pangs of the enjoyment, which has consumed the southern nation, perhaps all the Latin races, since the Renaissance.

It is a lapse back, back to the original position, the Mosiac position, of the divinity of the flesh, and the absoluteness of its laws. But also there is the Aphrodite-worship. The flesh, the senses, are now self-conscious. They know their aim. Their aim is in supreme sensation. They seek the maximum of sensation. They seek the reduction of the flesh, the flesh reacting upon itself, to a crisis, an ecstasy, a phosphorescent transfiguration in ecstasy.

The mind, all the time, subserves the senses. As in a cat, there is subtlety and beauty and the dignity of the darkness. But the fire is cold, as in the eyes of a cat, it is a green fire. It is fluid, electric. At its maximum it is the white ecstasy of phosphorescence, in the darkness, always amid the darkness, as under the black fur of a cat. Like the feline fire, it is destructive, always consuming and reducing to the ecstasy of sensation, which is the end in itself.

There is the I, always the I. And the mind is submerged, overcome. But the senses are superbly arrogant. The senses are the absolute, the god-like. For I can never have another man's senses. These are me, my senses absolutely me. And all

that is can only come to me through my senses. So that all is me, and is administered unto me. The rest, that is not me, is nothing, it is something which is nothing. So the Italian, through centuries, has avoided our Northern purposive industry, because it has seemed to him a form of nothingness.

It is the spirit of the tiger. The tiger is the supreme manifestation of the senses made absolute. This is the

> *Tiger, tiger, burning bright,*
> *In the forests of the night*

of Blake. It does indeed burn within the darkness. But the *essential* fire of the tiger is cold and white, a white ecstasy. It is seen in the white eyes of the blazing cat. This is the supremacy of the flesh, which devours all, and becomes transfigured into a magnificent brindled flame, a burning bush indeed.

This is one way of transfiguration into the eternal flame, the transfiguration through ecstasy in the flesh. Like the tiger in the night, I devour all flesh, I drink all blood, until this fuel blazes up in me to the consummate fire of the Infinite. In the ecstasy I am Infinite, I become again the great Whole, I am a flame of the One White Flame which is the Infinite, the Eternal, the Originator, the Creator, the Everlasting God. In the sensual ecstasy, having drunk all blood and devoured all flesh, I am become again the eternal Fire, I am infinite.

This is the way of the tiger; the tiger is supreme. His head is flattened as if there were some great weight on the hard skull, pressing, pressing, pressing the mind into a stone, pressing it down under the blood, to serve the blood. It is the subjugate instrument of the blood. The will lies above the loins, as it were at the base of the spinal column, there is the living will, the living mind of the tiger, there in the slender loins. That is the node, there in the spinal cord.

So the Italian, so the soldier. This is the spirit of the soldier. He, too, walks with his consciousness concentrated at the base of the spine, his mind subjugated, submerged. The will of the soldier is the will of the great cats, the will to ecstasy in destruction, in absorbing life into his own life, always his own life supreme, till the ecstasy burst into the white, eternal flame, the Infinite, the Flame of the Infinite. Then he is satisfied, he has been consummated in the Infinite.

This is the true soldier, this is the immortal climax of the senses. This is the acme of the flesh, the one superb tiger who has devoured all living flesh, and now paces backwards and forwards in the cage of its own infinite, glaring with blind, fierce, absorbed eyes at that which is nothingness to it.

The eyes of the tiger cannot see, except with the light from within itself, by the light of its own desire. Its own white, cold light is so fierce that the other warm light of day is outshone, it is not, it does not exist. So the white eyes of the tiger gleam to a point of concentrated vision, upon that which does not exist. Hence its terrifying sightlessness. The something which I know I am is hollow space to its vision, offers no resistance to the tiger's looking. It can only see of me that which it knows I am, a scent, a resistance, a voluptuous solid, a struggling warm violence that it holds overcome, a running of hot blood between its jaws, a delicious pang of live flesh in the mouth. This is sees. The rest is not.

And what is the rest, that which is-not the tiger, that which the tiger is-not? What is this?

What is that which parted ways with the terrific eagle-like angel of the senses at the Renaissance? The Italians said, "We are one in the Father: we will go back." The Northern races said, "We are one in Christ: we will go on."

What is the consummation in Christ? Man knows satisfaction when he surpasses all conditions and becomes, to himself, consummate in the Infinite, when he reaches a state of infinity. In the supreme ecstasy of the flesh, the Dionysic ecstasy, he reaches this state. But how does it come to pass in Christ?

It is not the mystic ecstasy. The mystic ecstasy is a special sensual ecstasy, it is the senses satisfying themselves with a self-created object. It is self-projection into the self, the sensuous self satisfied in a projected self.

Blessed are the poor in spirit, for theirs is the kingdom of heaven.
Blessed are they which are persecuted for righteousness' sake, for theirs is the kingdom of heaven.

The kingdom of heaven is this Infinite into which we may be consummated, then, if we are poor in spirit or persecuted for righteousness' sake.

Whosoever shall smite thee on the right cheek, turn to him the other also.
Love your enemies, bless them that curse you, do good to them that hate you, and pray for them which despitefully use you, and persecute you.
Be ye therefore perfect, even as your Father which is in heaven is perfect.

To be perfect, to be one with God, to be infinite and eternal, what shall we do? We must turn the other cheek, and love our enemies.

Christ is the lamb which the eagle swoops down upon, the dove taken by the hawk, the deer which the tiger devours.

What then, if a man come to me with a sword, to kill me, and I do not resist him, but suffer his sword and the death from his sword, what am I? Am I greater than he, am I stronger than he? Do I know a consummation in the Infinite, I, the prey, beyond the tiger who devours me? By my nonresistance I have robbed him of his consummation. For a tiger knows no consummation unless he kill a violated and struggling prey. There is no consummation merely for the

butcher, nor for a hyena. I can rob the tiger of his ecstasy, his consummation, his very *raison d'être*, by my non-resistance. In my non-resistance the tiger is infinitely destroyed.

But I, what am I? "Be ye therefore perfect." Wherein am I perfect in this submission? Is there an affirmation, behind my negation, other than the tiger's affirmation of his own glorious infinity?

What is the Oneness to which I subscribe, I who offer no resistance in the flesh?

Have I only the negative ecstasy of being devoured, of becoming thus part of the Lord, the Great Moloch, the superb and terrible God? I have this also, this subject ecstasy of consummation. But is there nothing else?

The Word of the tiger is: my senses are supremely Me, and my senses are God in me. But Christ said: God is in the others, who are not-me. In all the multitude of the others is God, and this is the great God, greater than the God which is Me. God is that which is Not-Me.

And this is the Christian truth, a truth complementary to the pagan affirmation: "God is that which is Me."

God is that which is Not-Me. In realising the Not-Me I am consummated, I become infinite. In turning the other cheek I submit to God who is greater than I am, other than I am, who is in that which is not me. This is the supreme consummation. To achieve this consummation I love my neighbour as myself. My neighbour is all that is not me. And if I love all this, have I not become one with the Whole, is not my consummation complete, am I not one with God, have I not achieved the Infinite?

After the Renaissance the Northern races continued forward, to put into practice this religious belief in the God which is Not-Me. Even the idea of the saving of the soul was really negative: it was a question of escaping damnation. The Puritans made the last great attack on the God who is Me. When they beheaded Charles the First, the king by Divine Right, they destroyed, symbolically, for ever, the supremacy of the Me who am the image of God, the Me of the flesh, of the senses, Me, the tiger burning bright, me the king, the Lord, the aristocrat, me who am divine because I am the body of God.

After the Puritans, we have been gathering data for the God who is not-me. When Pope said: "Know then thyself, presume not God to scan, The proper study of mankind is Man," he was stating the proposition: A man is right, he is consummated, when he is seeking to know Man, the great abstract; and the method of knowledge is by the analysis, which is the destruction, of the Self. The proposition up to that time was, a man is the epitome of the universe. He has only to express himself, to fulfil his desires, to satisfy his supreme senses.

Now the change has come to pass. The individual man is a limited being, finite in himself. Yet he is capable of apprehending that which is not himself. "The proper study of mankind is Man." This is another way of saying, "Thou shalt love thy neighbour as thyself." Which means, a man is consummated in his knowledge of that which is not himself, the abstract Man. Therefore the consummation lies in seeking that other, in knowing that other. Whereas the Stuart proposition was: "A man is consummated in expressing his own Self."

The new spirit developed into the empirical and ideal systems of philosophy. Everything that is, is consciousness. And in every man's consciousness, Man is great and illimit-

able, whilst the individual is small and fragmentary. Therefore the individual must sink himself in the great whole of Mankind.

This is the spirituality of Shelley, the perfectibility of man. This is the way in which we fulfil the commandment, "Be ye therefore perfect, even as your Father which is in heaven is perfect." This is Saint Paul's, "Now I know in part; but then shall I know even as I am known."

When a man knows everything and understands everything, then he will be perfect, and life will be blessed. He is capable of knowing everything and understanding everything. Hence he is justified in his hope of infinite freedom and blessedness.

The great inspiration of the new religion was the inspiration of freedom. When I have submerged or distilled away my concrete body and my limited desires, when I am like the skylark dissolved in the sky yet filling heaven and earth with song, then I am perfect, consummated in the Infinite. When I am all that is not-me, then I have perfect liberty, I know no limitation. Only I must eliminate the Self.

It was this religious belief which expressed itself in science. Science was the analysis of the outer self, the elementary substance of the self, the outer world. And the machine is the great reconstructed selfless power. Hence the active worship to which we were given at the end of the last century, the worship of mechanised force.

Still we continue to worship that which is not-me, the

Selfless world, though we would fain bring in the Self to help us. We are shouting the Shakespearean advice to warriors: "Then simulate the action of the tiger." We are trying to become again the tiger, the supreme, imperial, warlike Self. At the same time our ideal is the selfless world of equity.

We continue to give service to the Selfless God, we worship the great selfless oneness in the spirit, oneness in service of the great humanity, that which is Not-Me. This selfless God is He Who works for all alike, without consideration. And His image is the machine which dominates and cows us, we cower before it, we run to serve it. For it works for all humanity alike.

At the same time, we want to be warlike tigers. That is the horror: the confusing of the two ends. We warlike tigers fit ourselves out with machinery, and our blazing tiger wrath is emitted through a machine. It is a horrible thing to see machines hauled about by tigers, at the mercy of tigers, forced to express the tiger. It is a still more horrible thing to see tigers caught up and entangled and torn in machinery. It is horrible, a chaos beyond chaos, an unthinkable hell.

The tiger is not wrong, the machine is not wrong, but we, liars, lip-servers, duplicate fools, we are unforgivably wrong. We say: "I will be a tiger because I love mankind; out of love for other people, out of selfless service to that which is not me, I will even become a tiger." Which is absurd. A tiger devours because it is consummated in devouring, it achieves its absolute self in devouring. It does not devour because its unselfish conscience bids it do so, for the sake of the other deer and doves, or the other tigers.

Having arrived at the one extreme of mechanical selflessness, we immediately embrace the other extreme of the transcendent Self. But we try to be both at once. We do not cease to be the one before we become the other. We do not even play the rôles in turn. We want to be the tiger and the deer both in one. Which is just ghastly nothingness. We try to say, "The tiger is the lamb and the lamb is the tiger." Which is nil, nihil, nought.

The padrone took me into a small room almost contained in the thickness of the wall. There the Signora's dark eyes glared with surpise and agitation, seeing me intrude. She is younger than the Signore, a mere village tradesman's daughter, and, alas, childless.

It was quite true, the door stood open. Madame put down the screw-driver and drew herself erect. Her eyes were a flame of excitement. This question of a door-spring that made the door fly open when it should make it close roused a vivid spark in her soul. It was she who was wrestling with the angel of mechanism.

She was about forty years old, and flame-like and fierily sad. I think she did not know she was sad. But her heart was eaten by some impotence in her life.

She subdued her flame of life to the little padrone. He was strange and static, scarcely human, ageless, like a monkey. She supported him with her flame, supported his static,

ancient, beautiful form, kept in intact. But she did not believe in him.

Now, the Signora Gemma held her husband together whilst he undid the screw that fixed the spring. If they had been alone, she would have done it, pretending to be under his direction. But since I was there, he did it himself; a grey, shaky, highly-bred little gentleman, standing on a chair with a long screw-driver, whilst his wife stood behind him, her hands half-raised to catch him if he should fall. Yet he was strangely absolute, with a strange, intact force in his breeding.

They had merely adjusted the strong spring to the shut door, and stretched it slightly in fastening it to the door-jamb, so that it drew together the moment the latch was released, and the door flew open.

We soon made it right. There was a moment of anxiety, the screw was fixed. And the door swung to. They were delighted. The Signora Gemma, who roused in me an electric kind of melancholy, clasped her hands together in ecstasy as the door swiftly shut itself.

"Ecco!" she cried, in her vibrating, almost warlike woman's voice: "Ecco!"

Her eyes were aflame as they looked at the door. She ran forward to try it herself. She opened the door expectantly, eagerly. Pouf! – it shut with a bang.

"Ecco!" she cried, her voice quivering like bronze, over-wrought but triumphant.

I must try also. I opened the door. Pouf! It shut with a bang. We all exclaimed with joy.

Then the Signor di Paoli turned to me, with a gracious, bland, formal grin. He turned his back slightly on the woman, and stood holding his chin, his strange horse-mouth grinning almost pompously at me. It was an affair of gentlemen. His wife disappeared as if dismissed. Then the padrone broke into cordial motion. We must drink.

He would show me the estate. I had already seen the

house. We went out by the glass doors on the left, into the domestic courtyard.

It was lower than the gardens round it, and the sunshine came through the trellised arches on to the flagstones, where the grass grew fine and green in the cracks, and all was deserted and spacious and still. There were one or two orange-tubs in the light.

Then I heard a noise, and there in the corner, among all the pink geraniums and the sunshine, the Signora Gemma sat laughing with a baby. It was a fair, bonny thing of eighteen months. The Signora was concentrated upon the child as he sat, stolid and handsome, in his little white cap, perched on a bench picking at the pink geraniums.

She laughed, bent forward her dark face out of the shadow, swift into a glitter of sunshine near the sunny baby, laughing again excitedly, making mother-noises. The child took no notice of her. She caught him swiftly into the shadow, and they were obscured; her dark head was against the baby's wool jacket, she was kissing his neck, avidly, under the creeper leaves. The pink geraniums still frilled joyously in the sunshine.

I had forgotten the padrone. Suddenly I turned to him enquiringly.

"The Signora's nephew," he explained, briefly, curtly, in a small voice. It was as if he were ashamed, or too deeply chagrined.

The woman had seen us watching, so she came across the sunshine with the child, laughing, talking to the baby, not coming out of her own world to us, not acknowledging us, except formally.

The Signor Pietro, queer old horse, began to laugh and neigh at the child, with strange, rancorous envy. The child twisted its face to cry. The Signora caught it away, dancing back a few yards from her old husband.

"I am a stranger," I said to her across the distance. "He is afraid of a stranger."

"No, no," she cried back, her eyes flaring up. "It is the man. He always cries at the men."

She advanced again, laughing and roused, with the child in her arms. Her husband stood as if overcast, obliterated. She and I and the baby, in the sunshine, laughed a moment. Then I heard the neighing, forced laugh of the old man. He would not be left out. He seemed to force himself forward. He was bitter, acrid with chagrin and obliteration, struggling as if to assert his own existence. He was nullified.

The woman also was uncomfortable. I could see she wanted to go away with the child, to enjoy him alone, with palpitating, pained enjoyment. It was her brother's boy. And the old padrone was as if nullified by her ecstasy over the baby. He held his chin, gloomy, fretful, unimportant.

He was annulled. I was startled when I realised it. It was as though his reality were not attested till he had a child. It was as if his *raison d'être* had been to have a son. And he had no children. Therefore he had no *raison d'être*. He was nothing, a shadow that vanishes into nothing. And he was ashamed, consumed by his own nothingness.

I was startled. This, then, is the secret to Italy's attraction for us, this phallic worship. To the Italian the phallus is the symbol of individual creative immortality, to each man his own Godhead. The child is but the evidence of the Godhead.

And this is why the Italian is attractive, supple, and beautiful, because he worships the Godhead in the flesh. We envy him, we feel pale and insignificant beside him. Yet at the same time we feel superior to him, as if he were a child and we adult.

Wherein are we superior? Only because we went beyond the phallus in the search of the Godhead, the creative origin. And we found the physical forces and the secrets of science.

We have exalted Man far above the man who is in each one of us. Our aim is a perfect humanity, a perfect and equable human consciousness, selfless. And we obtain it in the subjection, reduction, analysis, and destruction of the Self. So on we go, active in science and mechanics, and social reform.

But we have exhausted ourselves in the process. We have found great treasures, and we are now impotent to use them. So we have said: "What good are these treasures, they are vulgar nothings." We have said: "Let us go back from this adventuring, let us enjoy our own flesh, like the Italian." But our habit of life, our very constitution, prevents our being quite like the Italian. The phallus will never serve us as a Godhead, because we do not believe in it: no Northern race does.

Therefore, either we set ourselves to serve our children, calling them 'the future', or else we turn perverse and destructive, give ourselves joy in the destruction of the flesh.

The children are not the future. The living truth is the future. Time and people do not make the future. Retrogression is not the future. Fifty million children growing up purposeless, with no purpose save the attainment of their own individual desires, these are not the future, they are only a disintegration of the past. The future is in living, growing truth, in advancing fulfilment.

But it is no good. Whatever we do, it is within the greater will towards self-reduction and a perfect society, analysis on the one hand, and mechanical construction on the other. This will dominates us as a whole, and until the whole breaks down, the will must persist. So that now, continuing in the old, splendid will for a perfect selfless humanity, we have become inhuman and unable to help ourselves, we are but attributes of the great mechanised society we have created on our way to perfection. And this great mechanised society, being selfless, is pitiless. It works on mechanically and destroys us, it is our master and our God.

It is past the time to leave off, to cease entirely from what we are doing, and from what we have been doing for hundreds of years. It is past the time to cease seeking one Infinite, ignoring, striving to eliminate the other. The Infinite is twofold, the Father and the Son, the Dark and the Light, the Senses and the Mind, the Soul and the Spirit, the self and the not-self, the Eagle and the Dove, the Tiger and the Lamb. The consummation of man is twofold, in the Self and in Self-lessness. By great retrogression back to the source of darkness in me, the Self, deep in the senses, I arrive at the Original, Creative Infinite. By projection forth from myself, by the elimination of my absolute sensual self, I arrive at the Ultimate Infinite, Oneness in the Spirit. They are two Infinites, twofold approach to God. And man must know both.

But he must never confuse them. They are eternally separate. The lion shall never lie down with the lamb. The lion eternally shall devour the lamb, the lamb eternally shall be devoured. Man knows the great consummation in the flesh, the sensual ecstasy, and that is eternal. Also the spiritual ecstasy of unanimity, that is eternal. But the two are separate and never to be confused. To neutralise the one with the other is unthinkable, an abomination. Confusion is horror and nothingness.

The two Infinites, negative and positive, they are always related, but they are never identical. They are always opposite, but there exists a relation between them. This is the Holy Ghost of the Christian Trinity. And it is this, the relation which is established between the two Infinites, the two natures of God, which we have transgressed, forgotten, sinned against. The Father is the Father, and the Son is the Son. I may know the Son and deny the Father, or know the Father and deny the Son. But that which I may never deny, and which I have denied, is the Holy Ghost which relates the dual Infinites into One Whole, which relates and keeps distinct the dual natures of God. To say that the two are one, this is the inadmissable lie. The two are related, by the intervention of the Third, into a Oneness.

There are two ways, there is not only One. There are two opposite ways to consummation. But that which relates them, like the base of the triangle, this is the constant, the Absolute, this makes the Ultimate Whole. And in the Holy Spirit I know the Two Ways, the Two Infinites, the Two Consummations. And knowing the Two, I admit the Whole. But excluding One, I exclude the Whole. And confusing the two, I make nullity, nihil.

"Mais," said the Signor, starting from his scene of ignominy, where his wife played with another man's child, "mais – voulez-vous vous promener dans mes petites terres?"

It came out fluently, he was so much roused in self-defence and self-assertion.

We walked under the pergola of bony vine-stocks, secure in the sunshine within the walls, only the long mountain, parallel with us, looking in.

I said how I liked the big vine-garden. I asked when it ended. The pride of the padrone came back with a click. He pointed me to the terrace, to the great shut lemon-houses above. They were all his. But – he shrugged his Italian shoulders – it was nothing, just a little garden, vous savez, monsieur. I protested it was beautiful, that I loved it, and that it seemed to me *very* large indeed. He admitted that today, perhaps, it was beautiful.

"Perchè – parceque – il fait un tempo – cosi – très bell' – très beau, ecco!"

He alighted on the word "beau" hurriedly, like a bird coming to ground with a little bounce.

The terraces of the garden are held up to the sun, the sun falls full upon them, they are like a vessel slanted up, to catch the superb, heavy light. Within the walls we are remote, perfect, moving in heavy spring sunshine, under the bony avenue of vines. The padrone makes little exclamatory noises that mean nothing, and teaches me the names of vegetables. The land is rich and black.

Opposite us, looking down on our security, is the long, arched mountain of snow. We climbed one flight of steps, and we could see the little villages on the opposite side of the lake. We climbed again, and could see the water rippling.

We came to a great stone building that I had thought was a storehouse, for open-air storage, because the walls are open half-way up, showing the darkness inside and the corner pillar very white and square and distinct in front of it.

Entering carelessly into the dimness, I started, for at my feet was a great floor of water, clear and green in its obscurity, going down between the walls, a reservoir in the gloom. The Signore laughed at my surprise. It was for irrigating the land, he said. It stank, slightly, with a raw smell; otherwise, I said,

what a wonderful bath it would make. The old Signore gave his little neighing laugh at the idea.

Then we climbed into a great loft of leaves, ruddy brown, stored in a great bank under the roof, seeming to give off a little red heat, as they gave off the lovely perfume of the hills. We passed through, and stood at the foot of the lemon-house. The big, blind building rose high in the sunshine before us.

All summer long, upon the mountain slopes steep by the lake, stand the rows of naked pillars rising out of the green foliage like ruins of temples: white, square pillars of masonry, standing forlorn in their colonnades and squares, rising up the mountain-sides here and there, as if they remained from some great race that had once worshipped here. And still, in the winter, some are seen, standing away in lonely places where the sun streams full, grey rows of pillars rising out of a broken wall, tier above tier, naked to the sky, forsaken.

They are the lemon plantations, and the pillars are to support the heavy branches of the trees, but finally to act as scaffolding of the great wooden houses that stand blind and ugly, covering the lemon trees in the winter.

In November, when cold winds came down and snow had fallen on the mountains, from out of the storehouses the men were carrying timber, and we heard the clang of falling planks. Then, as we walked along the military road on the mountain-side, we saw below, on the top of the lemon gardens, long, thin poles laid from pillar to pillar, and we heard

the two men talking and singing as they walked across perilously, placing the pales. In their clumsy zoccoli they strode easily across, though they had twenty or thirty feet to fall if they slipped. But the mountain-side, rising steeply, seemed near, and above their heads the rocks glowed high into the sky, so that the sense of elevation must have been taken away. At any rate, they went easily from pillar-summit to pillar-summit, with a great cave of space below. Then again was the rattle and clang of planks being laid in order, ringing from the mountain-side over the blue lake, till a platform of timber, old and brown, projected from the mountain-side, a floor when seen from above, a hanging roof when seen from below. And we, on the road above, saw the men sitting easily on this flimsy hanging platform, hammering the planks. And all day long the sound of hammering echoed among the rocks and olive woods, and came, a faint, quick concussion, to the men on the boats far out. When the roofs were on they put in the fronts, blocked in between the white pillars with old, dark wood, in roughly made panels. And here and there, at irregular intervals, was a panel of glass, pane overlapping pane in the long strip of narrow window. So that now these enormous, unsightly buildings bulge out on the mountain-sides, rising in two or three receding tiers, blind, dark, sordid-looking places.

In the morning I often lie in bed and watch the sunrise. The lake lies dim and milky, the mountains are dark blue at the back, while over them the sky gushes and glistens with light. At a certain place on the mountain ridge the light burns gold, seems to fuse a little groove on the hill's rim. It fuses and fuses at this point, till of a sudden it comes, the intense, molten, living light. The mountains melt suddenly, the light steps down, there is a glitter, a spangle, a clutch of spangles, a great unbearable sun-track flashing across the milky lake, and the light falls on my face. Then, looking aside, I hear the little slotting noise which tells me they are opening the lemon gardens, a long panel here and there, a long slot of darkness at irregular intervals between the brown wood and the glass stripes.

"Voulez-vous" – the Signor bows me in with outstretched hand – "voulez-vous entrer, monsieur?"

I went into the lemon-house, where the poor trees seem to mope in the darkness. It is an immense, dark, cold place. Tall lemon trees, heavy with half-visible fruit, crowd together, and rise in the gloom. They look like ghosts in the darkness of the underworld, stately, and as if in life, but only grand shadows of themselves. And lurking here and there, I see one of the pillars. But he, too, seems a shadow, not one of the dazzling white fellows I knew. Here we are, trees, men, pillars, the dark earth, the sad black paths, shut in in this enormous box. It is true, there are long strips of window and slots of space, so that the front is striped, and an occasional beam of light fingers the leaves of an enclosed tree and the sickly round lemons. But it is nevertheless very gloomy.

"But it is much colder in here than outside," I said.

"Yes," replied the Signor, "now. But at night – I think – "

I almost wished it were night to try. I wanted to imagine the trees cosy. They seemed now in the underworld. Between the lemon trees, beside the path, were little orange trees, and dozens of oranges hanging like hot coals in the twilight. When I warm my hands at them the Signor breaks me off one twig after another, till I have a bunch of burning oranges among dark leaves, a heavy bouquet. Looking down the Hades of the lemon-house, the many ruddy-clustered oranges beside the path remind me of the lights of a village along the lake at night, while the pale lemons above are the stars. There is a subtle, exquisite scent of lemon flowers. Then I notice a citron. He hangs heavy and bloated upon so small a tree, that he seems a dark green enormity. There is a great host of lemons overhead, half-visible, a swarm of ruddy oranges by the paths, and here and there a fat citron. It is almost like being under the sea.

At the corners of the path were round little patches of ash and stumps of charred wood, where fires had been kindled inside the house on cold nights. For during the second and third weeks in January the snow came down so low on the mountains that, after climbing for an hour, I found myself in a snow lane, and saw olive orchards on lawns of snow.

The padrone says that all lemons and sweet oranges are grafted on a bitter-orange stock. The plants raised from seed, lemon and sweet orange, fell prey to disease, so the cultivators found it safe only to raise the native bitter orange, and then to graft upon it.

And the maestra – she is the schoolmistress, who wears black gloves while she teaches us Italian – says that the lemon was brought by St. Francis of Assisi, who came to the Garda here and founded a church and a monastery. Certainly the church of San Francesco is very old and dilapidated, and its cloisters have some beautiful and original carvings of leaves and fruit upon the pillars, which seem to connect San Francesco with the lemon. I imagine him wandering here with a lemon in his pocket. Perhaps he made lemonade in the hot summer. But Bacchus had been before him in the drink trade.

Looking at his lemons, the Signore sighed. I think he hates them. They are leaving him in the lurch. They are sold retail at a halfpenny each all the year round. "But that is as dear, or dearer, than in England," I say. "Ah, but," says the maestra, "that is because your lemons are outdoor fruit from Sicily. Però – one of our lemons is as good as two from elsewhere."

It is true these lemons have an exquisite fragrance and perfume, but whether their force as lemons is double that of an ordinary fruit is a question. Oranges are sold at fourpence halfpenny the kilo – it comes about five for twopence, small ones. The citrons are sold also by weight in Salò for the making of that liqueur known as "Cedro". One citron fetches sometimes a shilling or more, but then the demand is necessarily small. So that it is evident, from these figures, the Lago di Garda cannot afford to grow its lemons much longer. The gardens are already many of them in ruins, and still more "Da Vendere".

We went out of the shadow of the lemon-house on to the roof of the section below us. When we came to the brink of the roof I sat down. The padrone stood behind me, a shabby, shaky little figure on his roof in the sky, a little figure of dilapidation, dilapidated as the lemon-houses themselves.

We were always level with the mountain-snow opposite. A film of pure blue was on the hills to the right and the left. There had been a wind, but it was still now. The water breathed an iridescent dust on the far shore, where the villages were groups of specks.

On the low level of the world, on the lake, an orange-sailed boat leaned slim to the dark-blue water, which had flecks of foam. A woman went down-hill quickly, with two goats and a sheep. Among the olives a man was whistling.

"Voyez," said the padrone, with distant, perfect melancholy. "There was once a lemon garden also there – you see the short pillars, cut off to make a pergola for the vine. Once there were twice as many lemons as now. Now we must have vine instead. From that piece of land I had two hundred lire a year, in lemons. From the vine I have only eighty."

"But wine is a valuable crop," I said.

"Ah – così-così! For a man who grows much. For me – poco, poco – peu."

Suddenly his face broke into a smile of profound melancholy, almost a grin, like a gargoyle. It was the real Italian melancholy, very deep, static.

"Vous voyez, monsieur – the lemon, it is all the year, all the year. But the vine – one crop – ?"

He lifts his shoulders and spreads his hands with that gesture of finality and fatality, while his face takes the blank, ageless look of misery, like a monkey's. There is no hope. There is the present. Either that is enough, the present, or there is nothing.

I sat and looked at the lake. It was beautiful as paradise, as the first creation. On the shores were the ruined lemon-pillars standing out in melancholy, the clumsy, enclosed lemon-houses seemed ramshackle, bulging among vine stocks and olive trees. The villages, too, clustered upon their churches, seemed to belong to the past. They seemed to be lingering in bygone centuries.

"But it is very beautiful," I protested. "In England – "

"Ah, in England," exclaimed the padrone, the same ageless monkey-like grin of fatality, tempered by cunning, coming on his face, "in England you have the wealth – les richesses – you have the mineral coal and the machines, vous savez. Here, we have the sun – "

He lifted his withered hand to the sky, to the wonderful source of that blue day, and he smiled, in histrionic triumph. But his triumph was only histrionic. The machines were more to his soul than the sun. He did not know these mechanisms, their great, human-contrived, inhuman power, and he wanted to know them. As for the sun, that is common property, and no man is distinguished by it. He wanted machines, machine-production, money, and human power. He wanted to know the joy of man who has got the earth in his grip, bound it up with railways, burrowed it with iron fingers, subdued it. He wanted this last triumph of the ego, this last reduction. He wanted to go where the English have gone, beyond the Self, into the great inhuman Not-Self, to create the great unliving creators, the machines, out of the active forces of nature that existed before flesh.

But he is too old. It remains for the young Italian to embrace his mistress, the machine.

I sat on the roof of the lemon-house, with the lake below and the snowy mountain opposite, and looked at the ruins on the old, olive-fuming shores, at all the peace of the ancient world still covered in sunshine, and the past seemed to me so lovely that one must look towards it, backwards, only backwards, where there is peace and beauty and no more dissonance.

I thought of England, the great mass of London, and the black, fuming, laborious Midlands and north-country. It seemed horrible. And yet, it was better than the padrone, this old, monkey-like cunning of fatality. It is better to go forward into error than to stay fixed inextricably in the past.

Yet what should become of the world? There was London and the industrial counties spreading like a blackness over all the world, horrible, in the end destructive. And the Garda was so lovely under the sky of sunshine, it was intolerable. For away, beyond, beyond all the snowy Alps, with the iridescence of eternal ice above them, was this England, black and foul and dry, with her soul worn down, almost worn away. And England was conquering the world with her machines and her horrible destruction of natural life. She was conquering the whole world.

And yet, was she not herself finished in this work? She had had enough. She had conquered the natural life to the end: she was replete with the conquest of the outer world, satisfied with the destruction of the Self. She would cease, she would turn round; or else expire.

If she still lived, she would begin to build her knowledge into a great structure of truth. There it lay, vast masses of rough-hewn knowledge, vast masses of machines and appliances, vast masses of ideas and methods, and nothing done with it, only teeming swarms of disintegrated human beings seething and perishing rapidly away amongst it, till it seems as if a world will be left covered with huge ruins, and scored by strange devices of industry, and quite dead, the people disappeared, swallowed up in the last efforts towards a perfect, selfless society.

ON THE
LAGO DI GARDA
THE THEATRE

DURING CARNIVAL A COMPANY IS PLAYING IN THE theatre. On Christmas Day the padrone came in with the key of his box, and would we care to see the drama? The theatre was small, a mere nothing, in fact; a mere affair of peasants, you understand; and the Signor di Paoli spread his hands and put his head on one side, parrot-wise; but we might find a little diversion – un peu de divertiment. With this he handed me the key.

I made suitable acknowledgments, and was really impressed. To be handed the key of a box at the theatre, so simply and pleasantly, in the large sitting-room looking over the grey lake of Christmas Day; it seemed to me a very graceful event. The key had a chain and a little shield of bronze, on which was beaten out a large figure 8.

So the next day we went to see I Spettri, expecting some good, crude melodrama. The theatre is an old church. Since that triumph of the deaf and dumb, the cinematograph, has come to give us the nervous excitement of speed, – grimace, agitation, and speed, as of flying atoms, chaos, – many an old church in Italy has taken a new lease of life.

This cast-off church made a good theatre. I realised how cleverly it had been constructed for the dramatic presentation of religious ceremonies. The east end is round, the walls are windowless, sound is well distributed. Now everything is theatrical, except the stone floor and two pillars at the back of the auditorium, and the slightly ecclesiastical seats below.

There are two tiers of little boxes in the theatre, some forty in all, with fringe and red velvet, and lined with dark red paper, quite like real boxes in a real theatre. And the padrone's is one of the best. It just holds three people.

We paid our threepence entrance fee in the stone hall and went upstairs. I opened the door of Number 8, and we were shut in our little cabin, looking down on all the world. Then I found the barber, Luigi, bowing profusely in a box opposite. It was necessary to make bows all round: ah, the chemist, on the upper tier, near the barber; how-do-you-do to the padrona of the hotel, who is our good friend, and who sits, wearing a little beaver shoulder-cape, a few boxes off; very cold salutation to the stout village magistrate with the long brown beard, who leans forward in the box facing the stage, while a grouping of faces look out from behind him; a warm smile to the family of the Signora Gemma, across next to the stage. Then we are settled.

I cannot tell why I hate the village magistrate. He looks like a family portrait by a Flemish artist, he himself weighing down the front of the picture with his portliness and his long brown beard, whilst the faces of his family are arranged in two groups for the background. I think he is angry at our intrusion. He is very republican and self-important. But we eclipse him easily, with the aid of a large black velvet hat, and black furs, and our Sunday clothes.

Downstairs the villagers are crowding, drifting like a heavy current. The women are seated, by church instinct, all

together on the left, with perhaps an odd man at the end of a row, beside his wife. On the right, sprawling in the benches, are several groups of bersaglieri, in grey uniforms and slanting cock's-feather hats; then peasants, fishermen, and an odd couple or so of brazen girls taking their places on the men's side.

At the back, lounging against the pillars or standing very dark and sombre, are the more reckless spirits of the village. Their black felt hats are pulled down, their cloaks are thrown over their mouths, they stand very dark and isolated in their moments of stillness, they shout and wave to each other when anything occurs.

The men are clean, their clothes are all clean washed. The rags of the poorest porter are always well washed. But it is Sunday to-morrow, and they are shaved only on a Sunday. So that they have a week's black growth on their chins. But they have dark, soft eyes, unconscious and vulnerable. They move and balance with loose, heedless motion upon their clattering zoccoli, they lounge with wonderful ease against the wall at the back, or against the two pillars, unconscious of the patches on their clothes or of their bare throats, that are knotted perhaps with a scarlet rag. Loose and abandoned, they lounge and talk, or they watch with wistful absorption the play that is going on.

They are strangely isolated in their own atmosphere, and as if revealed. It is as if their vulnerable being was exposed and they have not the wit to cover it. There is a pathos of physical sensibility and mental inadequacy. Their mind is not sufficiently alert to run with their quick, warm senses.

The men keep together, as if to support each other, the women also are together; in a hard, strong herd. It is as if the power, the hardness, the triumph, even in this Italian village, were with the women in their relentless, vindictive unity.

That which drives men and women together, the indomitable necessity, is like a bondage upon the people. They submit as under compulsion, under constraint. They come together mostly in anger and in violence of destructive passion. There is no comradeship between men and women, none whatsoever, but rather a condition of battle, reserve, hostility.

On Sundays the uncomfortable, excited, unwilling youth walks for an hour with his sweetheart, at a little distance from her, on the public highway in the afternoon. This is a concession to the necessity for marriage. There is no real courting, no happiness of being together, only the roused excitement which is based on a fundamental hostility. There is very little flirting, and what there is is of the subtle, cruel kind, like a sex duel. On the whole, the men and women avoid each other, almost shun each other. Husband and wife are brought together in a child, which they both worship. But in each of them there is only the great reverence for the infant, and the reverence for fatherhood or motherhood, as the case may be; there is no spiritual love.

In marriage, husband and wife wage the subtle, satisfying war of sex upon each other. It gives a profound satisfaction, a profound intimacy. But it destroys all joy, all unanimity in action.

On Sunday afternoons the uncomfortable youth walks by the side of his maiden for an hour in the public highway. Then he escapes; as from a bondage he goes back to his men companions. On Sunday afternoons and evenings the married woman, accompanied by a friend or by a child – she dare not go alone, afraid of the strange, terrible sex-war between her and the drunken man – is seen leading home the wine-drunken, liberated husband. Sometimes she is beaten when she gets home. It is part of the process. But there is no synthetic love between men and women, there is only passion, and passion is fundamental hatred, the act of love is a fight.

The child, the outcome, is divine. Here the union, the oneness, is manifest. Though spirit strove with spirit, in mortal conflict, during the sex-passion, yet the flesh united with flesh in oneness. The phallus is still divine. But the spirit, the mind of man, this has become nothing.

So the women triumph. They sit down below in the theatre, their perfectly dressed hair gleaming, their backs very straight, their heads carried tensely. They are not very noticeable. They seem held in reserve. They are just as tense and stiff as the men are slack and abandoned. Some strange will holds the women taut. They seem like weapons, dangerous. There is nothing charming nor winning about them; at the best a full, prolific maternity, at the worst a yellow poisonous bitterness of the flesh that is like a narcotic. But they are too strong for the men. The male spirit, which would subdue the immediate flesh to some conscious or social purpose, is overthrown. The woman in her maternity is the law-giver, the supreme authority. The authority of the man, in work, in public affairs, is something trivial in comparison. The pathetic ignominy of the village male is complete on Sunday afternoon, on his great day of liberation, when he is accompanied home, drunk but sinister, by the erect, unswerving, slightly cowed woman. His drunken terrorising is only pitiable, she is so obviously the more constant power.

And this is why the men must go away to America. It is not the money. It is the profound desire to rehabilitate themselves, to recover some dignity as men, as producers, as workers, as creators from the spirit, not only from the flesh. It is a profound desire to get away from women altogether, the terrible subjugation to sex, the phallic worship.

The company of actors in the little theatre was from a small town away on the plain, beyond Brescia. The curtain rose, everybody was still, with that profound, naïve attention which children give. And after a few minutes I realised that

I *Spettri* was Ibsen's *Ghosts*. The peasants and fishermen of the Garda, even the rows of ungovernable children, sat absorbed in watching as the Norwegian drama unfolded itself.

The actors are peasants. The leader is the son of a peasant proprietor. He is qualified as a chemist, but is unsettled, vagrant, prefers play-acting. The Signor Pietro di Paoli shrugs his shoulders and apologises for their vulgar accent. It is all the same to me. I am trying to get myself to rights with the play, which I have just lately seen in Munich, perfectly produced and detestable.

It was such a change from the hard, ethical, slightly mechanised characters in the German play, which was as perfect an interpretation as I can imagine, to the rather pathetic notion of the Italian peasants, that I had to wait to adjust myself.

The mother was a pleasant, comfortable woman harassed by something, she did not quite know what. The pastor was a ginger-haired caricature imitated from the northern stage, quite a lay figure. The peasants never laughed, they watched solemnly and absorbedly like children. The servant was just a slim, pert, forward hussy, much too flagrant. And then the son, the actor-manager: he was a dark, ruddy man, broad and thick-set, evidently of peasant origin, but with some education now; he was the important figure, the play was his.

And he was strangely disturbing. Dark, ruddy, and powerful, he could not be the blighted son of "Ghosts", the hectic, unsound, northern issue of a diseased father. His flashy Italian passion for his half-sister was real enough to make one uncomfortable: something he wanted and would have in spite of his own soul, something which fundamentally he did not want.

It was this contradiction within the man that made the play so interesting. A robust, vigorous man of thirty-eight, flaunting and florid as a rather successful Italian can be, there was yet a secret sickness which oppressed him. But it was no taint in the blood, it was rather a kind of debility in the soul. That which he wanted and would have, the sensual excitement, in his soul he did not want it, no, not at all. And yet he must act from his physical desires, his physical will.

His true being, his real self, was impotent. In his soul he was dependent, forlorn. He was childish and dependent on the mother. To hear him say, "Grazia, mamma!" would have tormented the mother-soul in any woman living. Such a child crying in the night! And for what?

For he was hot-blooded, healthy, almost in his prime, and free as a man can be in his circumstances. He had his own way, he admitted no thwarting. He governed his circumstances pretty much, coming to our village with his little company, playing the plays he chose himself. And yet, that which he would have he did not vitally want, it was only a sort of inflamed obstinacy that made him so insistent, in the masculine way. He was not going to be governed by women, he was not going to be dictated to in the least by any one. And this because he was beaten by his own flesh.

His real man's soul, the soul that goes forth and builds up a new world out of the void, was ineffectual. It could only revert to the senses. His divinity was the phallic divinity. The other male divinity, which is the spirit that fulfils in the world the new germ of an idea, this was denied and obscured in him, unused. And it was this spirit which cried out helplessly in him through the insistent, inflammable flesh. Even this play-acting was a form of physical gratification for him, it had in it neither real mind nor spirit.

It was so different from Ibsen, and so much more moving. Ibsen is exciting, nervously sensational. But this was really moving, a real crying in the night. One loved the Italian nation, and wanted to help it with all one's soul. But when one sees the perfect Ibsen, how one hates the Norwegian and Swedish nations! They are detestable.

They seem to be fingering with the mind the secret places and sources of the blood, impertinent, irreverent, nasty. There is a certain intolerable nastiness about the real Ibsen: the same thing is in Strindberg and in most of the Norwegian and Swedish writings. It is with them a sort of phallic worship also, but now the worship is mental and perverted: the phallus is the real fetish, but it is the source of uncleanliness and corruption and death, it is the Moloch, worshipped in obscenity.

Which is unbearable. The phallus is a symbol of creative divinity. But it represents only part of creative divinity. The Italian has made it represent the whole. Which is now his misery, for he has to destroy his symbol in himself.

Which is why the Italian men have the enthusiasm for war, unashamed. Partly it is the true phallic worship, for the phallic principle is to absorb and dominate all life. But also it is a desire to expose themselves to death, to know death, that death may destroy in them this too strong dominion of the blood, may once more liberate the spirit of outgoing, of uniting, of making order out of chaos, in the outer world, as the flesh makes a new order from chaos in begetting a new life, set them free to know and serve a greater idea.

The peasants below sat and listened intently, like children who hear and do not understand, yet who are spellbound. The children themselves sit spellbound on the benches till the play is over. They do not fidget or lose interest. They watch with wide, absorbed eyes at the mystery, held in thrall by the sound of emotion.

But the villagers do not really care for Ibsen. They let it go. On the feast of Epiphany, as a special treat, was given a poetic drama by D'Annunzio, *La Fiaccola sotto il Moggio – The Light under the Bushel*.

It is a foolish romantic play of no real significance. There are several murders and a good deal of artificial horror. But it is all a very nice and romantic piece of make-believe, like a charade.

So the audience loved it. After the performance of *Ghosts* I saw the barber, and he had the curious grey clayey look of an Italian who is cold and depressed. The sterile cold inertia, which the so-called passionate nations know so well, had

settled on him, and he went obliterating himself in the street, as if he were cold, dead.

But after the D'Annunzio play he was like a man who has drunk sweet wine and is warm.

"Ah, bellissimo, bellissimo!" he said, in tones of intoxicated reverence, when he saw me.

"Better than I Spettri?" I said.

He half-raised his hands, as if to imply the fatuity of the question.

"Ah, but – " he said, "it was D'Annunzio. The other . . ."

"That was Ibsen – a great Norwegian," I said, "famous all over the world."

"But, you know – D'Annunzio is a poet – oh, beautiful, beautiful!" There was no going beyond this "bello – bellissimo."

It was the language which did it. It was the Italian passion for rhetoric, for the speech which appeals to the senses and makes no demand on the mind. When an Englishman listens to a speech he wants at least to imagine that he understands thoroughly and impersonally what is meant. But an Italian only cares about the emotion. It is the movement, the physical effect of the language upon the blood which gives him supreme satisfaction. His mind is scarcely engaged at all. He is like a child, hearing and feeling without understanding. It is

the sensuous gratification he asks for. Which is why D'Annunzio is a god in Italy. He can control the current of the blood with his words, and although much of what he says is bosh, yet the hearer is satisfied, fulfilled.

Carnival ends on the 5th of February, so each Thursday there is a Serata d'Onore of one the actors. The first, and the only one for which prices were raised – to a fourpence entrance fee instead of threepence – was for the leading lady. The play was The Wife of the Doctor, a modern piece, sufficiently uninteresting; the farce that followed made me laugh.

Since it was her Evening of Honour, Adelaida was the person to see. She is very popular, though she is no longer young. In fact, she is the mother of the young pert person of Ghosts.

Nevertheless, Adelaida, stout and blonde and soft and pathetic, is the real heroine of the theatre, the prima. She is very good at sobbing; and afterwards the men exclaim involuntarily, out of their strong emotion, "bella, bella!" The women say nothing. They sit stiffly and dangerously as ever. But, no doubt, they quite agree this is the true picture of ill-used, tear-stained woman, the bearer of many wrongs. Therefore they take unto themselves the homage of the men's "bella, bella!" that follows the sobs: it is due recognition of their hard wrongs: "the woman pays." Nevertheless, they despise in their souls the plump, soft Adelaida.

Dear Adelaida, she is irreproachable. In every age, in every clime, she is dear, at any rate to the masculine soul, this soft, tear-blenched, blonde, ill-used thing. She must be ill-used and unfortunate. Dear Gretchen, dear Desdemona, dear Iphigenia, dear Dame aux Camélias, dear Lucy of Lammermoor, dear Mary Magdalene, dear, pathetic, unfortunate soul, in all ages and lands, how we love you. In the theatre she blossoms forth, she is the lily of the stage. Young and inexperienced as I am, I have broken my heart over her several times. I could write a sonnet-sequence to her, yes, the fair, pale, tear-stained thing, white-robed, with her hair down her back; I could call her by a hundred names, in a hundred languages, Mélisande, Elizabeth, Juliet, Butterfly, Phèdre, Minnehaha, etc. Each new time I hear her voice, with its faint clang of tears, my heart grows big and hot, and my bones melt. I detest her, but it is no good. My heart begins to swell like a bud under the plangent rain.

The last time I saw her was here, on the Garda, at Salò. She was the chalked, thin-armed daughter of Rigoletto. I detested her, her voice had a chalky squeak in it. And yet, by the end, my heart was over-ripe in my breast, ready to burst with loving affection. I was ready to walk on to the stage, to wipe out the odious, miscreant lover, and to offer her all myself, saying, "I can see it is real *love* you want, and you shall have it: I will give it to you."

Of course I know the secret of the Gretchen magic; it is all in the "Save me, Mr. Hercules!" phrase. Her shyness, her timidity, her trustfulness, her tears foster my own strength and grandeur. I am the positive half of the universe. But so I am, if it comes to that, just as positive as the other half.

Adelaida is plump, and her voice has just that moist, plangent strength which gives one a real voluptuous thrill. The moment she comes on the stage and looks round – a bit scared – she is *she*, Electra, Isolde, Sieglinde, Marguerite. She wears a dress of black voile, like the lady who weeps at the trial in the police-court. This is her modern uniform. Her antique garment is of trailing white, with a blonde pigtail and a flower. Realistically, it is black voile and a handkerchief.

Adelaida always has a handkerchief. And still I cannot resist it. I say, "There's the hanky!" Nevertheless, in two minutes it has worked its way with me. She squeezes it in her poor, plump hand as the tears begin to rise; Fate, or man, is inexorable, so cruel. There is a sob, a cry; she presses the fist and the hanky to her eyes, one eye, then the other. She weeps real tears, tears shaken from the depths of her soft, vulnerable, victimised female self. I cannot stand it. There I sit in the padrone's little red box and stifle my emotion, whilst I repeat in my heart: "What a shame, child, what a shame!" She is twice my age, but what is age in such a circumstance? "Your poor little hanky, its sopping. There, then, don't cry. It'll be all right. *I'll* see you're all right. *All* men are not beasts, you know." So I cover her protectively in my arms, and soon I shall be kissing her, for comfort, in the heat and prowess of my compassion, kissing her soft, plump cheek and neck closely, bringing my comfort nearer and nearer.

It is a pleasant and exciting rôle for me to play. Robert Burns did the part to perfection:

> O wert thou in the cauld blast
> On yonder lea, on yonder lea.

How many times does one recite that to all the Ophelias and Gretchens in the world:

> Thy bield should be my bosom.

How one admires one's bosom in that capacity! Looking down at one's shirt-front, one is filled with strength and pride.

Why are the women so bad at playing this part in real life, this Ophelia-Gretchen rôle? Why are they so unwilling to go mad and die for our sakes? They do it regularly on the stage.

But perhaps, after all, we write the plays. What a villain I am, what a black-browed, passionate, ruthless, masculine villain I am to the leading lady on the stage; and, on the other hand, dear heart, what a hero, what a fount of chivalrous generosity and faith! I am *anything* but a dull and law-abiding citizen. I am a Galahad, full of purity and spirituality, I am the Lancelot of valour and lust; I fold my hands, or I cock my hat

on one side, as the case may be: I am *myself*. Only, I am not a respectable citizen, not that, in this hour of my glory and my escape.

Dear Heaven, how Adelaida wept, her voice plashing like violin music, at my ruthless, masculine cruelty. Dear heart, how she sighed to rest on my sheltering bosom! And how I enjoyed my dual nature! How I admired myself!

Adelaida chose *La Moglie del Dottore* for her Evening of Honour. During the following week came a little storm of coloured bills: "Great Evening of Honour of Enrico Persevalli."

This is the leader, the actor-manager. What should he choose for his great occasion, this broad, thick-set, ruddy descendant of the peasant proprietors of the plain? No one knew. The title of the play was not revealed.

So we were staying at home, it was cold and wet. But the maestra came inflammably on that Thursday evening, and were we not going to the theatre, to see *Amleto*?

Poor maestra, she is yellow and bitter-skinned, near fifty, but her dark eyes are still corrosively inflammable. She was engaged to a lieutenant in the cavalry, who got drowned when she was twenty-one. Since then she has hung on the tree unripe, growing yellow and bitter-skinned, never developing.

"*Amleto!*" I say. "*Non lo conosco.*"

A certain fear comes into her eyes. She is schoolmistress, and has a mortal dread of being wrong.

"Si," she cries, wavering, appealing, "una dramma inglese."

"English!" I repeated.

"Yes, an English drama."

"How do you write it?"

Anxiously, she gets a pencil from her reticule, and, with black-gloved scrupulousness, writes *Amleto*.

"*Hamlet!*" I exclaim wonderingly.

"Ecco, *Amleto!*" cries the maestra, her eyes aflame with thankful justification.

Then I knew that Signor Enrico Persevalli was looking to me for an audience. His Evening of Honour would be a bitter occasion to him if the English were not there to see his performance.

I hurried to get ready, I ran through the rain. I knew he would take it badly that it rained on his Evening of Honour. He counted himself a man who had fate against him.

"Sono un disgraziato, io."

I was late. The First Act was nearly over. The play was not yet alive, neither in the bosoms of the actors nor in the audience. I closed the door of the box softly, and came forward. The rolling Italian eyes of Hamlet glanced up at me. There came a new impulse over the Court of Denmark.

Enrico looked a sad fool in his melancholy black. The doublet sat close, making him stout and vulgar, the knee-breeches seemed to exaggerate the commonness of his thick, rather short, strutting legs. And he carried a long black rag, as a cloak, for histrionic purposes. And he had on his face a portentous grimace of melancholy and philosophic importance. His was the caricature of Hamlet's melancholy self-absorption.

I stooped to arrange my footstool and compose my countenance. I was trying not to grin. For the first time, attired in philosophic melancholy of black silk, Enrico looked a boor and a fool. His close-cropped, rather animal head was common above the effeminate doublet, his sturdy, ordinary figure looked absurd in a melancholic droop.

All the actors alike were out of their element. Their Majesties of Denmark were touching. The Queen, burly little peasant woman, was ill at ease in her pink satin. Enrico had had no mercy. He knew she loved to be the scolding servant or housekeeper, with her head tied up in a handkerchief, shrill and vulgar. Yet here she was pranked out in an expanse of satin, la Regina. Regina, indeed!

She obediently did her best to be important. Indeed, she rather fancied herself; she looked sideways at the audience, self-consciously, quite ready to be accepted as an imposing and noble person, if they would esteem her such. Her voice sounded hoarse and common, but whether it was the pink satin in contrast, or a cold, I do not know. She was almost childishly afraid to move. Before she began a speech she looked down and kicked her skirt viciously, so that she was sure it was under control. Then she let go. She was a burly, downright little body of sixty, one rather expected her to box Hamlet on the ears.

Only she liked being a queen when she sat on the throne. There she perched with great satisfaction, her train splendidly displayed down the steps. She was as proud as a child, and she looked like Queen Victoria of the Jubilee period.

The King, her noble consort, also had new honours thrust upon him, as well as new garments. His body was real enough, but it had nothing at all to do with his clothes. They established a separate identity by themselves. But wherever he went, they went with him, to the confusion of everybody.

He was a thin, rather frail-looking peasant, pathetic, and very gentle. There was something pure and fine about him, he was so exceedingly gentle and by natural breeding courteous. But he did not feel kingly, he acted the part with beautiful, simple resignation.

Enrico Persevalli had overshot himself in every direction, but worst of all in his own. He had become a hulking fellow, crawling about with his head ducked between his shoulders, pecking and poking, creeping about after other people, sniffing at them, setting traps for them, absorbed by his own self-important self-consciousness. His legs, in their black knee-breeches, had a crawling, slinking look; he always carried the black rag of a cloak, something for him to twist about as he twisted in his own soul, overwhelmed by a sort of inverted perversity.

I had always felt an aversion from Hamlet: a creeping, unclean thing he seems, on the stage, whether he is Forbes Robertson or anybody else. His nasty poking and sniffing at his mother, his setting traps for the King, his conceited perversion with Ophelia make him always intolerable. The character is repulsive in its conception, based on self-dislike and a spirit of disintegration.

There is, I think, this strain of cold dislike, or self-dislike, through much of the Renaissance art, and through all the later Shakespeare. In Shakespeare it is a kind of corruption in the flesh and a conscious revolt from this. A sense of corruption in the flesh makes Hamlet frenzied, for he will never admit that it is his own flesh. Leonardo da Vinci is the same, but Leonardo loves the corruption maliciously. Michael Angelo rejects any feeling of corruption, he stands by the flesh, the flesh only. It is the corresponding reaction, but in the opposite direction. But that is all four hundred years ago. Enrico Persevalli has just reached the position. He is Hamlet, and evidently he has great satisfaction in the part. He is the modern Italian, suspicious, isolated, self-nauseated, labouring in a sense of physical corruption. But he will not admit it is in himself. He creeps about in self-conceit, transforming his own self-loathing. With what satisfaction did he reveal corruption – corruption in his neighbours he gloated in – letting his mother know he had discovered her incest, her uncleanness, gloated in torturing the incestuous King. Of all the unclean ones, Hamlet was the uncleanest. But he accused only the others.

Except in the "great" speeches, and there Enrico was betrayed, Hamlet suffered the extremity of physical self-loathing, loathing of his own flesh. The play is the statement of the most significant philosophic position of the Renaissance. Hamlet is far more even than Orestes, his prototype, a mental creature, anti-physical, anti-sensual. The whole drama is the tragedy of the convulsed reaction of the mind from the flesh, of the spirit from the self, the reaction from the great aristocratic to the great democratic principle.

An ordinary instinctive man, in Hamlet's position, would either have set about murdering his uncle, by reflex action, or else would have gone right away. There would have been no need for Hamlet to murder his mother. It would have been sufficient blood-vengeance if he had killed his uncle. But that is the statement according to the aristocratic principle.

Orestes was in the same position, but the same position two thousand years earlier, with two thousand years of experience wanting. So that the question was not so intricate in

him as in Hamlet, he was not nearly so conscious. The whole Greek life was based on the idea of the supremacy of the self, and the self was always male. Orestes was his father's child, he would be the same whatever mother he had. The mother was but the vehicle, the soil in which the paternal seed was planted. When Clytemnestra murdered Agamemnon, it was as if a common individual murdered God, to the Greek.

But Agamemnon, King and Lord, was not infallible. He was fallible. He had sacrificed Iphigenia for the sake of glory in war, for the fulfilment of the superb idea of self, but on the other hand he had made cruel dissension for the sake of the concubines captured in war. The paternal flesh was fallible, ungodlike. It lusted after meaner pursuits than glory, war, and slaying, it was not faithful to the highest idea of the self. Orestes was driven mad by the furies of his mother, because of the justice that they represented. Nevertheless he was in the end exculpated. The third play of the trilogy is almost

foolish, with its prating gods. But it means that, according to the Greek conviction, Orestes was right and Clytemnestra entirely wrong. But for all that, the infallible King, the infallible male Self, is dead in Orestes, killed by the furies of Clytemnestra. He gains his peace of mind after the revulsion from his own physical fallibility, but he will never be an unquestioned lord, as Agamemnon was. Orestes is left at peace, neutralised. He is the beginning of non-aristocratic Christianity.

Hamlet's father, the King, is, like Agamemnon, a warrior-king. But, unlike Agamemnon, he is blameless with regard to Gertrude. Yet Gertrude, like Clytemnestra, is the potential murderer of her husband, as Lady Macbeth is murderess, as the daughters of Lear. The women murder the supreme male, the ideal Self, the King and Father.

This is the tragic position Shakespeare must dwell upon. The woman rejects, repudiates the ideal Self which the male represents to her. The supreme representative, King and Father, is murdered by the Wife and the Daughters.

What is the reason? Hamlet goes mad in a revulsion of rage and nausea. Yet the women-murderers only represent some ultimate judgment in his own soul. At the bottom of his own soul Hamlet has decided that the Self in its supremacy, Father and King, must die. It is a suicidal decision for his involuntary soul to have arrived at. Yet it is inevitable. The great religious, philosophic tide, which had been swelling all through the Middle Ages, had brought him there.

The question, to be or not to be, which Hamlet puts himself, does not mean, to live or not to live. It is not the simple human being who puts himself the question, it is the supreme I, King and Father. To be or not to be King, Father, in the Self supreme? And the decision is, not to be.

It is the inevitable philosophic conclusion of all the Renaissance. The deepest impulse in man, the religious impulse, is the desire to be immortal, or infinite, consummated. And this impulse is satisfied in fulfilment of an idea, a steady progression. In this progression man is satisfied, he seems to have reached his goal, this infinity, this immortality, this eternal being, with every step nearer which he takes.

And so, according to his idea of fulfilment, man establishes the whole order of life. If my fulfilment is the fulfilment and establishment of the unknown divine Self which I am, then I shall proceed in the realising of the greatest idea of the self, the highest conception of the I, my order of life will be kingly, imperial, aristocratic. The body politic also will culminate in this divinity of the flesh, this body imbued with glory, invested with divine power and might, the King, the Emperor. In the body politic also I shall desire a king, an emperor, a tyrant, glorious, mighty, in whom I see myself consummated and fulfilled. This is inevitable!

But during the Middle Ages, struggling within this pagan, original transport, the transport of the Ego, was a small dissatisfaction, a small contrary desire. Amid the pomp of kings and popes was the Child Jesus and the Madonna. Jesus the

King gradually dwindled down. There was Jesus the Child, helpless, at the mercy of all the world. And there was Jesus crucified.

The old transport, the old fulfilment of the Ego, the Davidian ecstasy, the assuming of all power and glory unto the self, the becoming infinite through the absorption of all into the Ego, this gradually became unsatisfactory. This was not the infinite, this was not immortality. This was eternal death, this was damnation.

The monk rose up with his opposite ecstasy, the Christian ecstasy. There was a death to die: the flesh, the self, must die, so that the spirit should rise again immortal, eternal, infinite. I am dead unto myself, but I live in the Infinite. The finite Me is no more, only the Infinite, the Eternal, is.

At the Renaissance this great half-truth overcame the other great half-truth. The Christian Infinite, reached by a process of abnegation, a process of being absorbed, dissolved, diffused into the great Not-Self, supplanted the old pagan Infinite, wherein the self like a root threw out branches and radicles which embraced the whole universe, became the Whole.

There is only one Infinite, the world now cried, there is the great Christian Infinite of renunciation and consummation in the not-self. The other, that old pride, is damnation. The sin of sins is Pride, it is the way to total damnation. Whereas the pagans based their life on pride.

And according to this new Infinite, reached through re-nunciation and dissolving into the Others, the Neighbour, man must build up his actual form of life. With Savonarola and Martin Luther the living Church actually transformed itself, for the Roman Church was still pagan. Henry VIII. simply said: "There is no Church, there is only the State." But with Shakespeare the transformation had reached the State also. The King, the Father, the representative of the Consummate Self, the maximum of all life, the symbol of the consummate being, the becoming Supreme, Godlike, Infinite, he must perish and pass away. This Infinite was not infinite, this consummation was not consummate, all this was fallible, false. It was rotten, corrupt. It must go. But Shakespeare was also the thing itself. Hence his horror, his frenzy, his self-loathing.

The King, the Emperor is killed in the soul of man, the old order of life is over, the old tree is dead at the root. So said Shakespeare. It was finally enacted in Cromwell. Charles I. took up the old position of kingship by divine right. Like Hamlet's father, he was blameless otherwise. But as representative of the old form of life, which mankind now hated with frenzy, he must be cut down, removed. It was a symbolic act.

The world, our world of Europe, had now really turned, swung round to a new goal, a new idea, the Infinite reached through the omission of Self. God is all that which is Not-Me. I am consummate when my Self, the resistant solid, is reduced and diffused into all that which is Not-Me:

my neighbour, my enemy, the great Otherness. Then I am perfect.

And from this belief the world began gradually to form a new State, a new body politic, in which the Self should be removed. There should be no king, no lords, no aristocrats. The world continued in its religious belief, beyond the French Revolution, beyond the great movement of Shelley and Godwin. There should be no Self. That which was supreme was that which was Not-Me, the other. The governing factor in the State was the idea of the good of others; that is, the Common Good. And the *vital* governing idea in the State has been this idea since Cromwell.

Before Cromwell the idea was "For the King," because every man saw himself consummated in the King. After Cromwell the idea was "For the good of my neighbour," or "For the good of the people," or "For the good of the whole." This has been our ruling idea, by which we have more or less lived.

Now this has failed. Now we say that the Christian Infinite is not infinite. We are tempted, like Nietzsche, to return back to the old pagan Infinite, to say that is supreme. Or we are inclined, like the English and the Pragmatist, to say, "There is no Infinite, there is no Absolute. The only Absolute is expediency, the only reality is sensation and momentariness." But we may say this, even act on it, *à la Sanine*. But we never believe it.

What is really Absolute is the mystic Reason which connects both Infinites, the Holy Ghost that relates both natures of God. If we now wish to make a living State, we must build it up to the idea of the Holy Spirit, the supreme Relationship. We must say, the pagan Infinite is infinite, the Christian Infinite is infinite: these are our two Consummations, in both of these we are consummated. But that which relates them alone is absolute.

This Absolute of the Holy Ghost we may call Truth or Justice or Right. These are partial names, indefinite and unsatisfactory unless there be kept the knowledge of the two Infinites, pagan and Christian, which they go between. When both are there, they are like a superb bridge, on which one can stand and know the whole world, my world, the two halves of the universe.

"Essere, o non essere, è qui il punto."

To be or not to be was the question for Hamlet to settle. It is no longer our question, at least, not in the same sense. When it is a question of death, the fashionable young suicide declares that his self-destruction is the final proof of his own incontrovertible being. And as for not-being in our public life, we have achieved it as much as ever we want to, as much as is necessary. Whilst in private life there is a swing back to paltry selfishness as a creed. And in the war there is the position of neutralisation and nothingness. It is a question of knowing how *to be*, and how *not to be*, for we must fulfil both.

Enrico Persevalli was detestable with his "Essere, o non essere." He whispered it in a hoarse whisper as if it were some melodramatic murder he was about to commit. As a matter of fact, he knows quite well, and has known all his life, that his pagan Infinite, his transport of the flesh and the supremacy of the male in fatherhood, is all unsatisfactory. All his life he has really cringed before the northern Infinite of the Not-Self, although he has continued in the Italian habit of Self. But it is mere habit, sham.

How can he know anything about being and not-being when he is only a maudlin compromise between them, and all he wants is to be a maudlin compromise? He is neither one nor the other. He has neither being nor not-being. He is as equivocal as the monks. He was detestable, mouthing Hamlet's sincere words. He has still to let go, to know what not-being is, before he can *be*. Till he has gone through the Christian negation of himself, and has known the Christian consummation, he is a mere amorphous heap.

For the soliloquies of Hamlet are as deep as the soul of man can go, in one direction, and as sincere as the Holy Spirit itself in their essence. But thank heaven, the bog into which Hamlet struggled is almost surpassed.

It is a strange thing, if a man covers his face, and speaks with his eyes blinded, how significant and poignant he becomes. The ghost of this Hamlet was very simple. He was wrapped down to the knees in a great white cloth, and over his face was an open-work woollen shawl. But the naïve blind helplessness and verity of his voice was strangely convincing. He seemed the most real thing in the play. From the knees downward he was Laertes, because he had on Laertes' white trousers and patent leather slippers. Yet he was strangely real, a voice out of the dark.

The Ghost is really one of the play's failures, it is so trivial and unspiritual and vulgar. And it was spoilt for me from the first. When I was a child I went to the twopenny travelling theatre to see *Hamlet*. The Ghost had on a helmet and a breastplate. I sat in pale transport.

"'Amblet, 'Amblet, I *am* thy father's ghost."

Then came a voice from the dark, silent audience, like a cynical knife to my fond soul:

"Why tha arena, I can tell thy voice."

The peasants loved Ophelia: she was in white with her hair down her back. Poor thing, she was pathetic, demented. And no wonder, after Hamlet's "O, that this too, too solid flesh would melt!" What then of her young breasts and her womb? Hamlet with her was a very disagreeable sight. The peasants loved her. There was a hoarse roar, half of indignation, half of roused passion, at the end of her scene.

The graveyard scene, too, was a great success, but I could not bear Hamlet. And the grave-digger in Italian was a mere buffoon. The whole scene was farcical to me because of the Italian, "Questo cranio, Signore – " And Enrico, dainty fellow, took the skull in a corner of his black cloak. As an Italian, he would not willingly touch it. It was unclean. But he looked a fool, hulking himself in his lugubriousness. He was as self-important as D'Annunzio.

The close fell flat. The peasants had applauded the whole graveyard scene wildly. But at the end of all they got up and crowded to the doors, as if to hurry away: this in spite of Enrico's final feat: he fell backwards, smack down three steps of the throne platform, on to the stage. But planks and braced muscle will bounce, and Signor Amleto bounced quite high again.

It was the end of *Amleto*, and I was glad. But I loved the theatre, I loved to look down on the peasants, who were so absorbed. At the end of the scenes the men pushed back their black hats, and rubbed their hair across their brows with a pleased excited movement. And the women stirred in their seats.

Just one man was with his wife and child, and he was of the same race as my old woman at San Tommaso. He was fair, thin, and clear, abstract, of the mountains. He seemed to have gathered his wife and child together into another, finer atmosphere, like the air of the mountains, and to guard them in it. This is the real Joseph, father of the child. He has a fierce, abstract look, wild and untamed as a hawk, but like a hawk at its own nest, fierce with love. He goes out and buys a tiny bottle of lemonade for a penny, and the mother and child sip it in tiny sips, whilst he bends over, like a hawk arching its wings.

It is the fierce spirit of the Ego come out of the primal infinite, but detached, isolated, an aristocrat. He is not an Italian, dark-blooded. He is fair, keen as steel, with the blood of the mountaineer in him. He is like my old spinning woman. It is curious how, with his wife and child, he makes a little separate world down there in the theatre, like a hawk's nest, high and arid under the gleaming sky.

The Bersaglieri sit close together in groups, so that there is a strange, corporal connection between them. They have close-cropped, dark, slightly bestial heads, and thick shoulders, and thick brown hands on each other's shoulders. When an act is over they pick up their cherished hats and fling on their cloaks and go into the hall. They are rather rich, the Bersaglieri.

They are like young, half-wild oxen, such strong, sturdy, dark lads, thickly built and with strange hard heads, like young male caryatides. They keep close together, as if there were some physical instinct connecting them. And they are quite womanless. There is a curious inter-absorption among themselves, a sort of physical trance that holds them all, and puts their minds to sleep. There is a strange, hypnotic unanimity among them as they put on their plumed hats and go out together, always very close, as if their bodies must touch. Then they feel safe and content in this heavy, physical trance. They are in love with one another, the young men love the young men. They shrink from the world beyond, from the outsiders, from all who are not Bersaglieri of their barracks.

One man is a sort of leader. He is very straight and solid, solid like a wall, with a dark, unblemished will. His cock-feathers slither in a profuse, heavy stream from his black oil-cloth hat, almost to his shoulder. He swings round. His feathers slip in a cascade. Then he goes out to the hall, his feather tossing and falling richly. He must be well off. The Bersaglieri buy their own black cock's-plumes, and some pay twenty or thirty francs for the bunch, so the maestra said. The poor ones have only poor, scraggy plumes.

There is something very primitive about these men. They remind me really of Agamemnon's soldiers clustered on the seashore, men, all men, a living, vigorous, physical host of men. But there is a pressure on these Italian soldiers, as if they were men caryatides, with a great weight on their heads, making their brain hard, asleep, stunned. They all look as if their real brain were stunned, as if there were another centre of physical consciousness from which they lived.

Separate from them all is Pietro, the young man who lounges on the wharf to carry things from the steamer. He starts up from sleep like a wild-cat as somebody claps him on the shoulder. It is the start of a man who has many enemies. He is almost an outlaw. Will he ever find himself in prison? He is the *gamin* of the village, well detested.

He is twenty-four years old, thin, dark, handsome, with a cat-like lightness and grace, and a certain repulsive, *gamin* evil in his face. Where everybody is so clean and tidy, he is almost ragged. His week's beard shows very black in his slightly hollow cheeks. He hates the man who has waked him by clapping him on the shoulder.

Pietro is already married, yet he behaves as if he were not. He has been carrying on with a loose woman, the wife of the citron-coloured barber, the Siciliano. Then he seats himself on the women's side of the theatre, behind a young person from Bogliaco, who also has no reputation, and makes her talk to him. He leans forward, resting his arms on the seat before him, stretching his slender, cat-like, flexible loins. The padrona of the hotel hates him – "ein frecher Kerl," she says with contempt, and she looks away. Her eyes hate to see him.

In the village there is the clerical party, which is the majority; there is the anti-clerical party, and there are the ne'er-do-wells. The clerical people are dark and pious and cold; there is a curious stone-cold, ponderous darkness over them, moral and gloomy. Then the anti-clerical party, with the Syndaco at the head, is bourgeois and respectable as far as the middle-aged people are concerned, banal, respectable, shut off as by a wall from the clerical people. The young anti-clericals are the young bloods of the place, the men who gather every night in the more expensive and less-respectable café. These young men are all free-thinkers, great dancers, singers, players of the guitar. They are immoral and slightly cynical. Their leader is the young shopkeeper, who has lived in Vienna, who is a bit of a bounder, with a veneer of sneering irony on an original good nature. He is well-to-do, and gives dances to which only the looser women go, with these reckless young men. He also gets up parties of pleasure, and is chiefly responsible for the coming of the players to the theatre this carnival. These young men are disliked, but they belong to the important class, they are well-to-do, and they have the life of the village in their hands. The clerical peasants are priest-ridden and good, because they are poor and afraid and superstitious. There is, lastly, a sprinkling of loose women, one who keeps the inn where the soldiers drink. These women are a definite set. They know what they are, they pretend nothing else. They are not prostitutes, but just loose women. They keep to their own clique, among men and women, never wanting to compromise anybody else.

And beyond all these there are the Franciscan friars in their brown robes, so shy, so silent, so obliterated, as they stand back in the shop, waiting to buy the bread for the monastery, waiting obscure and neutral, till no one shall be in the shop wanting to be served. The village women speak to them in a curious neutral, official, slightly contemptuous voice. They answer neutral and humble, though distinctly.

At the theatre, now the play is over, the peasants in their black hats and cloaks crowd the hall. Only Pietro, the wharf-lounger, has no cloak, and a bit of a cap on the side of his head instead of a black felt hat. His clothes are thin and loose on his thin, vigorous, cat-like body, and he is cold, but he takes no notice. His hands are always in his pockets, his shoulders slightly raised.

The few women slip away home. In the little theatre-bar the well-to-do young atheists are having another drink. Not that they spend much. A tumbler of wine or a glass of vermouth costs a penny. And the wine is horrible new stuff. Yet the little baker, Agostino, sits on a bench with his pale baby on his knee, putting the wine to its lips. And the baby drinks, like a blind fledgling.

Upstairs, the quality has paid its visits and shaken hands: the Syndaco and the well-to-do half-Austrian owners of the woodyard, the Bertolini, have ostentatiously shown their mutual friendship; our padrone, the Signor Pietro di Paoli, has visited his relatives the Graziani in the box next the stage, and has spent two intervals with us in our box; meanwhile, his two peasants standing down below, pathetic, thin contadini of the old school, like worn stones, have looked up at us as if we are the angels in heaven, with a reverential, devotional eye, they themselves far away below, standing in the bay at the back, below all.

The chemist and the grocer and the school-mistress pay calls. They have all sat self-consciously posed in the front of their boxes, like framed photographs of themselves. The second grocer and the baker visit each other. The barber looks in on the carpenter, then drops downstairs among the crowd. Class distinctions are cut very fine. As we pass with the padrona of the hotel, who is a Bavarian, we stop to speak to our own padroni, the Di Paoli. They have a warm handshake and effusive polite conversation for us; for Maria Samuelli, a distant bow. We realise our mistake.

The barber – not the Siciliano, but flashy little Luigi with the big tie-ring and the curls – knows all about the theatre. He says that Enrico Persevalli has for his mistress Carina, the servant in *Ghosts*: that the thin, gentle, old-looking king in *Hamlet* is the husband of Adelaida, and Carina is their daughter: that the old, sharp, fat little body of a queen is Adelaida's mother: that they all like Enrico Persevalli, because he is a very clever man: but that the "Comic," Il Brillante, Francesco, is unsatisfied.

In three performances in Epiphany week, the company took two hundred and sixty-five francs, which was phenomenal. The manager, Enrico Persevalli, and Adelaida pay twenty-four francs for every performance, or every evening on which a performance is given, as rent for the theatre, including light. The company is completely satisfied with its reception on the Lago di Garda.

So it is all over. The Bersaglieri go running all the way home, because it is already past half-past ten. The night is very dark. About four miles up the lake the searchlights of the Austrian border are swinging, looking for smugglers. Otherwise the darkness is complete.

ON THE
LAGO DI GARDA
SAN GAUDENZIO

I N THE AUTUMN THE LITTLE ROSY CYCLAMENS blossom in the shade of this west side of the lake. They are very cold and fragrant, and their scent seems to belong to Greece, to the Bacchae. They are real flowers of the past. They seem to be blossoming in the landscape of Phaedra and Helen. They bend down, they brood like little chill fires. They are little living myths that I cannot understand.

After the cyclamens the Christmas roses are in bud. It is at this season that the cacchi are ripe on the trees in the garden, whole naked trees full of lustrous, orange-yellow, paradisal fruit, gleaming against the wintry blue sky. The monthly roses still blossom frail and pink, there are still crimson and yellow roses. But the vines are bare and the lemon-houses shut. And then, in mid-winter, the lowest buds of the Christmas roses appear under the hedges and rocks and by the streams. They are very lovely, these first, large, cold, pure buds, like violets, like magnolias, but cold, lit up with the light from the snow.

The days go by, through the brief silence of winter, when the sunshine is so still and pure, like iced wine, and the dead leaves gleam brown, and water sounds hoarse in the ravines. It is so still and transcendent, the cypress trees poise like flames of forgotten darkness, that should have been blown out at the end of the summer. For as we have candles to light the darkness of night, so the cypresses are candles to keep the darkness aflame in the full sunshine.

Meanwhile, the Christmas roses become many. They rise from their budded, intact humbleness near the ground, they rise up, they throw up their crystal, they become handsome, they are heaps of confident, mysterious whiteness in the shadow of a rocky stream. It is almost uncanny to see them. They are the flowers of darkness, white and wonderful beyond belief.

Then their radiance becomes soiled and brown, they thaw, break, and scatter and vanish away. Already the primroses are coming out, and the almond is in bud. The winter is passing away. On the mountains the fierce snow gleams apricot gold as evening approaches, golden, apricot, but so bright that it is almost frightening. What can be so fiercely gleaming when all is shadowy? It is something inhuman and unmitigated between heaven and earth.

The heavens are strange and proud all the winter, their progress goes on without reference to the dim earth. The dawns come white and translucent, the lake is a moonstone in the dark hills, then across the lake there stretches a vein of fire, then a whole, orange, flashing track over the whiteness. There is the exquisite silent passage of the day, and then at evening the afterglow, a huge incandescence of rose, hanging above and gleaming, as if it were the presence of a host of angels in rapture. It gleams like a rapturous chorus, then passes away, and the stars appear, large and flashing.

Meanwhile, the primroses are dawning on the ground, their light is growing stronger, spreading over the banks and under the bushes. Between the olive roots the violets are out, large, white, grave violets, and less serious blue ones. And looking down the hill, among the grey smoke of olive leaves, pink puffs of smoke are rising up. It is the almond and the apricot trees, it is the Spring.

Soon the primroses are strong on the ground. There is a bank of small, frail crocuses shooting the lavender into this spring. And then the tussocks and tussocks of primroses are fully out, there is full morning everywhere on the banks and roadsides and stream-sides, and around the olive roots, a morning of primroses underfoot, with an invisible threading of many violets, and then the lovely blue clusters of hepatica, really like pieces of blue sky showing through a clarity of primrose. The few birds are piping thinly and shyly, the streams sing again, there is a strange flowering shrub full of incense, overturned flowers of crimson and gold, like Bohemian glass. Between the olive roots new grass is coming, day is leaping all clear and coloured from the earth, it is full Spring, full first rapture.

Does it pass away, or does it only lose its pristine quality? It deepens and intensifies, like experience. The days seem to be darker and richer, there is a sense of power in the strong air. On the banks by the lake the orchids are out, many, many pale bee-orchids standing clear from the short grass over the lake. And in the hollows are the grape hyacinths, purple as noon, with the heavy, sensual fragrance of noon. They are many-breasted, and full of milk, and ripe, and sun-darkened, like many-breasted Diana.

We could not bear to live down in the village any more, now that the days opened large and spacious and the evenings drew out in sunshine. We could not bear the indoors, when above us the mountains shone in clear air. It was time to go up, to climb with the sun.

So after Easter we went to San Gaudenzio. It was three miles away, up the winding mule-track that climbed higher and higher along the lake. Leaving the last house of the village, the path wound on the steep, cliff-like side of the lake, curving into the hollow where the landslip had tumbled the rocks in chaos, then out again on to the bluff of a headland that hung over the lake.

Thus we came to the tall barred gate of San Gaudenzio, on which was the usual little fire-insurance tablet, and then the advertisements for beer, "Birra, Verona," which is becoming a more and more popular drink.

Through the gate, inside the high wall, is the little Garden of Eden, a property of three or four acres fairly level upon a headland over the lake. The high wall girds it on the land side, and makes it perfectly secluded. On the lake side it is bounded by the sudden drops of the land, in sharp banks and terraces, overgrown with ilex and with laurel bushes, down to the brink of the cliff, so that the thicket of the first declivities seems to safeguard the property.

The pink farmhouse stands almost in the centre of the little territory, among the olive trees. It is a solid, six-roomed place, about fifty years old, having been rebuilt by Paolo's

uncle. Here we came to live for a time with the Fiori, Maria and Paolo, and their three children, Giovanni and Marco and Felicina.

Paolo had inherited, or partly inherited, San Gaudenzio, which had been in his family for generations. He was a peasant of fifty-three, very grey and wrinkled and worn-looking, but at the same time robust, with full strong limbs and a powerful chest. His face was old, but his body was solid and powerful. His eyes were blue like upper ice, beautiful. He had been a fair-haired man, now he was almost white.

He was strangely like the pictures of peasants in the northern Italian pictures, with the same curious nobility, the same aristocratic, eternal look of motionlessness, something statuesque. His head was hard and fine, the bone finely constructed, though the skin of his face was loose and furrowed with work. His temples had that fine, hard clarity which is seen in Mantegna, an almost jewel-like quality.

We all loved Paolo, he was so finished in his being, detached, with an almost classic simplicity and gentleness, an eternal kind of sureness. There was also something concluded and unalterable about him, something inaccessible.

Maria Fiori was different. She was from the plain, like Enrico Persevalli and the Bersaglieri from the Venetian district. She reminded me again of oxen, broad-boned and massive in

physique, dark-skinned, slow in her soul. But, like the oxen of the plain, she knew her work, she knew the other people engaged in the work. Her intelligence was attentive and purposive. She had been a housekeeper, a servant, in Venice and Verona, before her marriage. She had got the hang of this world of commerce and activity, she wanted to master it. But she was weighted down by her heavy animal blood.

Paolo and she were the opposite sides of the universe, the light and the dark. Yet they lived together now without friction, detached, each subordinated in their common relationship. With regard to Maria, Paolo omitted himself; Maria omitted herself with regard to Paolo. Their souls were silent and detached, completely apart, and silent, quite silent. They shared the physical relationship of marriage as if it were something beyond them, a third thing.

They had suffered very much in the earlier stages of their connection. Now the storm had gone by, leaving them, as it were, spent. They were both by nature passionate, vehement. But the lines of their passion were opposite. Hers was the primitive, crude, violent flux of the blood, emotional and undiscriminating, but wanting to mix and mingle. His was the hard, clear, invulnerable passion of the bones, finely tempered and unchangeable. She was the flint and he the steel.

But in continual striking together they only destroyed each other. The fire was a third thing, belonging to neither of them.

She was still heavy and full of desire. She was much younger than he.

"How long did you know your Signora before you were married?" she asked me.

"Six weeks," I said.

"Il Paolo e me, venti giorni, tre settimani," she cried vehemently. Three weeks they had known each other when they married. She still triumphed in the fact. So did Paolo. But it was past, strangely and rather terribly past.

What did they want when they came together, Paolo and she? He was a man over thirty, she was a woman of twenty-three. They were both violent in desire and of strong will. They came together at once, like two wrestlers almost matched in strength. Their meetings must have been splendid. Giovanni, the eldest child, was a tall lad of sixteen, with soft brown hair and grey eyes, and a clarity of brow, and the same calm simplicity of bearing which made Paolo so complete; but the son had at the same time a certain brownness of skin, a heaviness of blood, which he had from his mother. Paolo was so clear and translucent.

In Giovanni the fusion of the parents was perfect, he was a perfect spark from the flint and steel. There was in Paolo a subtle intelligence in feeling, a delicate appreciation of the other person. But the mind was unintelligent, he could not grasp a new order. Maria Fiori was much sharper and more adaptable to the ways of the world. Paolo had an almost glass-like quality, fine and clear and perfectly tempered; but he was also finished and brittle. Maria was much coarser, more vulgar, but also she was more human, more fertile, with crude potentiality. His passion was too fixed in its motion, hers too loose and overwhelming.

But Giovanni was beautiful, gentle, and courtly like Paolo, but warm, like Maria, ready to flush like a girl with anger or confusion. He stood straight and tall, and seemed to look into the far distance with his clear grey eyes. Yet also he could look at one and touch one with his look, he could meet one. Paolo's blue eyes were like the eyes of the old spinning-woman, clear and blue and belonging to the mountains, their vision seemed to end in space, abstract. They reminded me of the eyes of the eagle, which looks into the sun, and which teaches its young to do the same, although they are unwilling.

Marco, the second son was thirteen years old. He was his mother's favourite. Giovanni loved his father best. But Marco was his mother's son, with the same brown-gold and red complexion, like a pomegranate, and coarse black hair, and brown eyes like pebble, like agate, like an animal's eyes. He had the same broad, bovine figure, though he was only a boy. But there was some discrepancy in him. He was not unified, he had no identity.

He was strong and full of animal life, but always aimless, as though his wits scarcely controlled him. But he loved his

mother with a fundamental, generous, undistinguishing love. Only he always forgot what he was going to do. He was much more sensitive than Maria, more shy and reluctant. But his shyness, his sensitiveness only made him more aimless and awkward, a tiresome clown, slack and uncontrolled, witless. All day long his mother shouted and shrilled and scolded at him, or hit him angrily. He did not mind, he came up like a cork, warm and roguish and curiously appealing. She loved him with a fierce protective love, grounded on pain. There was such a split, a contrariety in his soul, one part reacting against the other, which landed him always into trouble.

It was when Marco was a baby that Paolo had gone to America. They were poor on San Gaudenzio. There were the few olive trees, the grapes, and the fruit; there was the one cow. But these scarcely made a living. Neither was Maria content with the real peasants' lot any more, polenta at midday and vegetable soup in the evening, and no way out, nothing to look forward to, no future, only this eternal present. She had been in service, and had eaten bread and drunk coffee, and known the flux and variable chance of life. She had departed from the old static conception. She knew what one might be, given a certain chance. The fixture was the thing she militated against. So Paolo went to America, to California, into the gold mines.

Maria wanted the future, the endless possibility of life on earth. She wanted her sons to be freer, to achieve a new plane of living. The peasant's life was a slave's life, she said, railing against the poverty and the drudgery. And it was quite true, Paolo and Giovanni worked twelve and fourteen hours a day at heavy laborious work that would have broken an Englishman. And there was nothing at the end of it. Yet Paolo was even happy so. This was the truth to him.

It was the mother who wanted things different. It was she who railed and railed against the miserable life of the peasants. When we were going to throw to the fowls a dry broken penny roll of white bread, Maria said, with anger and shame and resentment in her voice: "Give it to Marco, he will eat it. It isn't too dry for him."

White bread was a treat for them even now, when everybody eats bread. And Maria Fiori hated it, that bread should be a treat to her children, when it was the meanest food of all the rest of the world. She was in opposition to this order. She did not want her sons to be peasants, fixed and static as posts driven in the earth. She wanted them to be in the great flux of life, in the midst of all possibilities. So she at length sent Paolo to America to the gold-mines. Meanwhile, she covered the wall of her parlour with picture postcards, to bring the outer world of cities and industries into her house.

Paolo was entirely remote from Maria's world. He had not yet even grasped the fact of money, not thoroughly. He reckoned in land and olive trees. So he had the old fatalistic attitude to his circumstances, even to his food. The earth was the Lord's and the fulness thereof: also the leanness thereof. Paolo could only do his part and leave the rest. If he ate in plenty, having oil and wine and sausage in the house, and plenty of maize-meal, he was glad with the Lord. If he ate meagrely, of poor polenta, that was fate, it was the skies that ruled these things, and no man ruled the skies. He took his fate as it fell from the skies.

Maria was exorbitant about money. She would charge us all she could for what we had and for what was done for us.

Yet she was not mean in her soul. In her soul she was in a state of anger because of her own closeness. It was a violation to her strong animal nature. Yet her mind had wakened to the value of money. She knew she could alter her position, the position of her children, by virtue of money. She knew it was only money that made the difference between master and servant. And this was all the difference she would acknowledge. So she ruled her life according to money. Her supreme passion was to be mistress rather than servant, her supreme aspiration for her children was that in the end they might be masters and not servants.

Paolo was untouched by all this. For him there was some divinity about a master which even America had not destroyed. If we came in for supper whilst the family was still at table he would have the children at once take their plates to the wall, he would have Maria at once set the table for us, though their own meal were never finished. And this was not servility, it was the dignity of a religious conception. Paolo regarded us as belonging to the Signoria, those who are elect, near to God. And this was part of his religious service. His life was a ritual. It was very beautiful, but it made me unhappy, the purity of his spirit was so sacred and the actual facts seemed such a sacrilege to it. Maria was nearer to the actual truth when she said that money was the only distinction. But Paolo had hold of an eternal truth, where hers was temporal. Only Paolo misapplied this eternal truth. He should not have given Giovanni the inferior status and a fat, mean Italian tradesman the superior. That was false, a real falsity. Maria knew it and hated it. But Paolo could not distinguish between the accident of riches and the aristocracy of the spirit. So Maria rejected him altogether, and went to the other extreme. We were all human beings like herself; naked, there was no distinction between us, no higher nor lower. But we were possessed of more money than she. And she had to steer her course between these two conceptions. The money alone made the real distinction, the separation; the being, the life made the common level.

Paolo had the curious peasants' avarice also, but it was not meanness. It was a sort of religious conservation of his own power, his own self. Fortunately he could leave all business transactions on our account to Maria, so that his relation with us was purely ritualistic. He would have given me anything, trusting implicitly that I would fulfil my own nature as Signore, one of those more godlike, nearer the light of perfection than himself, a peasant. It was pure bliss to him to bring us the first-fruit of the garden, it was like laying it on an altar.

And his fulfilment was in a fine, subtle, exquisite relationship, not of manners, but subtle interappreciation. He worshipped a finer understanding and a subtler tact. A further fineness and dignity and freedom in bearing was to him an approach towards the divine, so he loved men best of all, they fulfilled his soul. A woman was always a woman, and sex was a low level whereon he did not esteem himself. But a man, a doer, the instrument of God, he was really godlike.

Paolo was a Conservative. For him the world was established and divine in its establishment. His vision grasped a small circle. A finer nature, a higher understanding, took in a greater circle, comprehended the whole. So that when Paolo was in relation to a man of further vision, he himself was extended towards the whole. Thus he was fulfilled. And his initial assumption was that every signore, every gentleman, was a man of further, purer vision than himself. This assumption was false. But Maria's assumption, that no one had a further vision, no one was more elect than herself, that we are all one flesh and blood and being, was even more false. Paolo was mistaken in actual life, but Maria was ultimately mistaken.

Paolo, conservative as he was, believing that a priest must be a priest of God, yet very rarely went to church. And he used the religious oaths that Maria hated, even *Porca-Maria*. He always used oaths, either Bacchus or God or Mary or the Sacrament. Maria was always offended. Yet it was she who, in her soul, jeered at the Church and at religion. She wanted the human society as the absolute, without religious abstractions. So Paolo's oaths enraged her, because of their profanity, she said. But it was really because of their subscribing to another superhuman order. She jeered at the clerical people. She made a loud clamour of derision when the parish priest of the village above went down to the big village on the lake, and across the piazza, the quay, with two pigs in a sack on his shoulder. This was a real picture of the sacred minister to her.

One day, when a storm had blown down an olive tree in front of the house, and Paolo and Giovanni were beginning

to cut it up, this same priest of Mugiano came to San Gauden-zio. He was an iron-grey, thin, disreputable-looking priest, very talkative and loud and queer. He seemed like an old ne'er-do-well in priests' black, and he talked loudly, almost to himself, as drunken people do. At once *he* must show the Fiori how to cut up the tree, he must have the axe from Paolo. He shouted to Maria for a glass of wine. She brought it out to him with a sort of insolent deference, insolent con-tempt of the man and traditional deference to the cloth. The priest drained the tumblerful of wine at one drink, his thin throat with its Adam's apple working. And he did not pay the penny.

Then he stripped off his cassock and put away his hat, and, a ludicrous figure in ill-fitting black knee-breeches and a not very clean shirt, and red handkerchief round his neck, he proceeded to give great extravagant blows at the tree. He was like a caricature. In the doorway Maria was encouraging him rather jeeringly, whilst she winked at me. Marco was stifling his hysterical amusement in his mother's apron, and pranc-ing with glee. Paolo and Giovanni stood by the fallen tree, very grave and unmoved, inscrutable, abstract. Then the youth came away to the doorway, with a flush mounting on his face and a grimace distorting its youngness. Only Paolo, unmoved and detached, stood by the tree with unchanging, abstract face, very strange, his eyes fixed in the ageless stare which is so characteristic.

Meanwhile the priest swung drunken blows at the tree, his thin buttocks bending in the green-black broadcloth, sup-ported on thin shanks, and thin throat growing dull purple in the red-knotted kerchief. Nevertheless he was doing the job. His face was wet with sweat. He wanted another glass of wine.

He took no notice of us. He was strangely a local, even a mountebank figure, but entirely local, an appurtenance of the district.

It was Maria who jeeringly told us the story of the priest, who shrugged her shoulders to imply that he was a con-temptible figure. Paolo sat with the abstract look on his face, as of one who hears and does not hear, is not really con-cerned. He never opposed or contradicted her, but stayed apart. It was she who was violent and brutal in her ways. But sometimes Paolo went into a rage, and then Maria, every-body, was afraid. It was a white heavy rage, when his blue eyes shone unearthly, and his mouth opened with a curious drawn blindness of the old Furies. There was something of the cruelty of a falling mass of snow, heavy, horrible. Maria drew away, there was a silence. Then the avalanche was finished.

They must have had some cruel fights before they learned to withdraw from each other so completely. They must have begotten Marco in hatred, terrible disintegrated opposition and otherness. And it was after this, after the child of their opposition was born, that Paolo went away to California, leaving his San Gaudenzio, travelling with several com-

panions, like blind beasts, to Havre, and thence to New York, then to California. He stayed five years in the gold-mines, in a wild valley, living with a gang of Italians in a town of corrugated iron.

All the while he had never really left San Gaudenzio. I asked him, "Used you to think of it, the lake, the Monte Baldo, the laurel trees down the slope?" He tried to see what I wanted to know. Yes, he said – but uncertainly. I could see that he had never been really homesick. It had been very wretched on the ship going from Havre to New York. That he told me about. And he told me about the gold-mines, the galleries, the valley, the huts in the valley. But he had never really fretted for San Gaudenzio whilst he was in California.

In real truth he was at San Gaudenzio all the time, his fate was riveted there. His going away was an excursion from reality, a kind of sleep-walking. He left his own reality there in the soil above the lake of Garda. That his body was in California, what did it matter? It was merely for a time, and for the sake of his own earth, his land. He would pay off the mortgage. But the gate at home was his gate all the time, his hand was on the latch.

As for Maria, he had felt his duty towards her. She was part of his little territory, the rooted centre of the world. He sent her home the money. But it did not occur to him, in his soul, to miss her. He wanted her to be safe with the children, that was all. In his flesh perhaps he missed the woman. But his spirit was even more completely isolated since marriage. Instead of having united with each other, they had made each other more terribly distinct and separate. He could live alone eternally. It was his condition. His sex was functional, like eating and drinking. To take a woman, a prostitute at the camp, or not to take her, was no more vitally important than to get drunk or not to get drunk of a Sunday. And fairly often on Sunday Paolo got drunk. His world remained unaltered.

But Maria suffered more bitterly. She was a young, powerful, passionate woman, and she was unsatisfied body and soul. Her soul's unsatisfaction became a bodily unsatisfaction. Her blood was heavy, violent, anarchic, insisting on the equality of the blood in all, and therefore on her own absolute right to satisfaction.

She took a wine licence for San Gaudenzio, and she sold wine. There were many scandals about her. Somehow it did not matter very much, outwardly. The authorities were too divided among themselves to enforce public opinion. Between the clerical party and the radicals and the socialists, what canons were left that were absolute? Besides, these wild villages had always been ungoverned.

Yet Maria suffered. Even she, according to her conviction, belonged to Paolo. And she felt betrayed, betrayed and deserted. The iron had gone deep into her soul. Paolo had deserted her, she had been betrayed to other men for five years. There was something cruel and implacable in life. She sat sullen and heavy, for all her quick activity. Her soul was sullen and heavy.

I could never believe Felicina was Paolo's child. She was an unprepossessing little girl, affected, cold, selfish, foolish. Maria and Paolo, with real Italian greatness, were warm and natural towards the child in her. But they did not love her in their very souls, she was the fruit of ash to them. And this must have been the reason that she was so self-conscious and foolish and affected, small child that she was.

Paolo had come back from America a year before she was born – a year before she was born, Maria insisted. The husband and wife lived together in a relationship of complete negation. In his soul he was sad for her, and in her soul she felt annulled. He sat at evening in the chimney-seat, smoking, always pleasant and cheerful, not for a moment thinking he was unhappy. It had all taken place in his subconsciousness. But his eyebrows and eyelids were lifted in a kind of vacancy, his blue eyes were round and somehow finished, though he was so gentle and vigorous in body. But the very quick of him was killed. He was like a ghost in the house, with his loose throat and powerful limbs, his open, blue extinct eyes, and his musical, slightly husky voice, that seemed to sound out of the past.

And Maria, stout and strong and handsome like a peasant woman, went about as if there were a weight on her, and her voice was high and strident. She, too, was finished in her life. But she remained unbroken, her will was like a hammer that destroys the old form.

Giovanni was patiently labouring to learn a little English. Paolo knew only four or five words, the chief of which were "a'right," "boss," "bread," and "day." The youth had these by heart, and was studying a little more. He was very graceful and lovable, but he found it difficult to learn. A confused light, like hot tears, would come into his eyes when he had again forgotten the phrase. But he carried the paper about with him, and he made steady progress.

He would go to America, he also. Not for anything would he stay in San Gaudenzio. His dream was to be gone. He would come back. The world was not San Gaudenzio to Giovanni.

The old order, the order of Paolo and of Pietro di Paoli, the aristocratic order of the supreme God, God the Father, the Lord, was passing away from the beautiful little territory. The household no longer receives its food, oil and wine and maize, from out of the earth in the motion of fate. The earth is annulled, and money takes its place. The landowner, who is the lieutenant of God and of Fate, like Abraham, he, too, is annulled. There is now the order of the rich, which supersedes the order of the Signoria.

It is passing away from Italy as it has passed from England. The peasant is passing away, the workman is taking his place.

The stability is gone. Paolo is a ghost, Maria is the living body. And the new order means sorrow for the Italian more even than it has meant for us. But he will have the new order.

San Gaudenzio is already becoming a thing of the past. Below the house, where the land drops in sharp slips to the sheer cliff's edge, over which it is Maria's constant fear that Felicina will tumble, there are the deserted lemon gardens of the little territory, snug down below. They are invisible till one descends by tiny paths, sheer down into them. And there they stand, the pillars and walls erect, but a dead emptiness prevailing, lemon trees all dead, gone, a few vines in their place. It is only twenty years since the lemon trees finally perished of a disease and were not renewed. But the deserted terrace, shut between great walls, descending in their openness full to the south, to the lake and the mountain opposite, seem more terrible than Pompeii in their silence and utter seclusion. The grape hyacinths flower in the cracks, the lizards run, this strange place hangs suspended and forgotten, forgotten for ever, its erect pillars utterly meaningless.

I used to sit and write in the great loft of the lemon house, high up, far, far from the ground, the open front giving across the lake and the mountain snow opposite flush with twilight. The old matting and boards, the old disused implements of lemon culture made shadows in the deserted place. Then there would come the call from the back, away above: "Venga, venga mangiare."

We ate in the kitchen, where the olive and laurel wood burned in the open fireplace. It was always soup in the evening. Then we played games or cards, all playing; or there was singing, with the accordion, and sometimes a rough mountain peasant with a guitar.

But it is all passing away. Giovanni is in America, unless he has come back to the War. He will not want to live in San Gaudenzio when he is a man, he says. He and Marco will not spend their lives wringing a little oil and wine out of the rocky soil, even if they are not killed in the fighting which is going on at the end of the lake. In my loft by the lemon houses now I should hear the guns. And Giovanni kissed me with a kind of supplication when I went on to the steamer, as if he were beseeching for a soul. His eyes were bright and clear and lit up with courage. He will make a good fight for the new soul he wants – that is, if they do not kill him in this War.

ON THE
LAGO DI GARDA
THE DANCE

ARIA HAD NO REAL LICENCE FOR SAN GAUDEN-
zio, yet the peasants always called for wine. It
is easy to arrange in Italy. The penny is paid
another time.

The wild old road that skirts the lake-side,
scrambling always higher as the precipice becomes steeper,
climbing and winding to the villages perched high up, passes
under the high boundary-wall of San Gaudenzio, between
that and the ruined church. But the road went just as much
between the vines and past the house as outside, under the
wall; for the high gates were always open, and men or
women and mules come into the property to call at the door
of the homestead. There was a loud shout, "Ah – a – a – ah –
Mari – 'a. O – O – Oh Pa'o'!" from outside, another wild, in-
articulate cry from within, and one of the Fiori appeared in
the doorway to hail the new-comer.

It was usually a man, sometimes a peasant from Mugiano,
high up, sometimes a peasant from the wilds of the
mountain, a wood-cutter, or a charcoal-burner. He came in
and sat in the house-place, his glass of wine in his hand between his knees, or on the floor between his feet, and he
talked in a few wild phrases, very shy, like a hawk indoors,
and unintelligible in his dialect.

Sometimes we had a dance. Then, for the wine to drink,
three men came with mandolines and guitars, and sat in a
corner playing their rapid tunes, while all danced on the
dusty brick floor of the little parlour. No strange women

were invited, only men; the young bloods from the big village on the lake, the wild men from above. They danced the
slow, trailing, lilting polka-waltz round and round the small
room, the guitars and mandolines twanging rapidly, the dust
rising from the soft bricks. There were only the two English
women: so men danced with men, as the Italians love to do.
They love even better to dance with men, with a dear blood-
friend, than with women.

"It's better like this, two men?" Giovanni says to me, his
blue eyes hot, his face curiously tender.

The wood-cutters and peasants take off their coats, their
throats are bare. They dance with strange intentness, particu-
larly if they have for partner an English Signora. Their feet in
thick boots are curiously swift and significant. And it is
strange to see the Englishwomen, as they dance with the
peasants, transfigured with a kind of brilliant surprise. All the
while the peasants are very courteous, but quiet. They see the
women dilate and flash, they think they have found a footing,
they are certain. So the male dancers are quiet, but even
grandiloquent, their feet nimble, their bodies wild and confident.

They are at a loss when the two English Signoras move together and laugh excitedly at the end of the dance.

"Isn't it fine?"

"Fine! Their arms are like iron, carrying you round."

"Yes! Yes! And the muscles on their shoulders! I never
knew there were such muscles! I'm almost frightened."

"But it's fine, isn't it? I'm getting into the dance."

"Yes – yes – you've only to let them take you."

Then the glasses are put down, the guitars give their strange, vibrant, almost painful summons, and the dance begins again.

It is a strange dance, strange and lilting, and changing as the music changed. But it had always a kind of leisurely dignity, a trailing kind of polka-waltz, intimate, passionate, yet never hurried, never violent in its passion, always becoming more intense. The women's faces changed to a kind of transported wonder, they were in the very rhythm of delight. From the soft bricks of the floor the red ochre rose in a thin cloud of dust, making hazy the shadowy dancers; the three musicians, in their black hats and their cloaks, sat obscurely in the corner, making a music that came quicker and quicker, making a dance that grew swifter and more intense, more subtle, the men seeming to fly and to implicate other strange inter-rhythmic dance into the women, the women drifting and palpitating as if their souls shook and resounded to a breeze that was subtly rushing upon them, through them; the men worked their feet, their thighs swifter, more vividly, the music came to an almost intolerable climax, there was a moment when the dance passed into a possession, the men caught up the women and swung them from the earth, leapt with them for a second, and then the next phase of the dance had begun, slower again, more subtly interwoven, taking perfect, oh, exquisite delight in every interrelated movement, a rhythm within a rhythm, a subtle approaching and drawing nearer to a climax, nearer, till, oh, there was the surpassing lift and swing of the women, when the woman's body seemed like a boat lifted over the powerful, exquisite wave of the man's body, perfect, for a moment, and then once more the slow, intense, nearer movement of the dance began, always nearer, nearer, always to a more perfect climax.

And the women waited as if in transport for the climax, when they would be flung into a movement surpassing all movement. They were flung, borne away, lifted like a boat on a supreme wave, into the zenith and nave of the heavens, consummate.

Then suddenly the dance crashed to an end, and the dancers stood stranded, lost, bewildered, on a strange shore. The air was full of red dust, half-lit by the lamp on the wall; the players in the corner were putting down their instruments to take up their glasses.

And the dancers sat round the wall, crowding in the little room, faint with the transport of repeated ecstasy. There was a subtle smile on the face of the men, subtle, knowing, so finely sensual that the conscious eyes could scarcely look at it. And the women were dazed, like creatures dazzled by too much light. The light was still on their faces, like a blindness, a reeling, like a transfiguration. The men were bringing wine, on a little tin tray, leaning with their proud, vivid loins, their faces flickering with the same subtle smile. Meanwhile, Maria Fiori was splashing water, much water, on the red floor.

There was the smell of water among the glowing, transfigured men and women who sat gleaming in another world, round the walls.

The peasants have chosen their women. For the dark, handsome Englishwoman, who looks like a slightly malignant Madonna, comes Il Duro; for the "bella bionda," the wood-cutter. But the peasants have always to take their turn after the young well-to-do men from the village below.

Nevertheless, they are confident. They cannot understand the middle-class diffidence of the young men who wear collars and ties and finger-rings.

The wood-cutter from the mountain is of medium height, dark, thin, and hard as a hatchet, with eyes that are black like the very flaming thrust of night. He is quite a savage. There is something strange about his dancing, the violent way he works one shoulder. He has a wooden leg, from the knee-joint. Yet he dances well, and is inordinately proud. He is fierce as a bird, and hard with energy as a thunderbolt. He

will dance with the blonde signora. But he never speaks. He is like some violent natural phenomenon rather than a person. The woman begins to wilt a little in his possession.

"E bello – il ballo?" he asks at length, one direct, flashing question.

"Si – molto bello," cries the woman, glad to have speech again.

The eyes of the wood-cutter flash like actual possession. He seems now to have come into his own. With all his senses, he is dominant, sure.

He is inconceivably vigorous in body, and his dancing is almost perfect, with a little catch in it, owing to his lameness, which brings almost a pure intoxication. Every muscle in his body is supple as steel, supple, as strong as thunder, and yet so quick, so delicately swift, it is almost unbearable. As he draws near to the swing, the climax, the ecstasy, he seems to lie in wait, there is a sense of a great strength crouching ready. Then it rushes forth, liquid, perfect, transcendent, the woman swoons over in the dance, and it goes on, enjoyment, infinite, incalculable enjoyment. He is like a god, a strange natural phenomenon, most intimate and compelling, wonderful.

But he is not a human being. The woman, somewhere shocked in her independent soul, begins to fall away from him. She has another being, which he has not touched, and which she will fall back upon. The dance is over, she will fall back on herself. It is perfect, too perfect.

During the next dance, while she is in the power of the educated Ettore, a perfect and calculated voluptuary, who knows how much he can get out of this Northern woman, and only how much, the wood-cutter stands on the edge of the darkness, in the open doorway, and watches. He is fixed upon her, established, perfect. And all the while she is aware of the insistent hawk-like poising of the face of the wood-cutter, poised on the edge of the darkness, in the doorway, in possession, unrelinquishing.

And she is angry. There is something stupid, absurd, in the hard, talon-like eyes watching so fiercely and so confidently in the doorway, sure, unmitigated. Has the creature no sense?

The woman reacts from him. For some time she will take no notice of him. But he waits, fixed. Then she comes near to him, and his will seems to take hold of her. He looks as her with a strange, proud, inhuman confidence, as if his influence with her was already accomplished.

"Venga – venga un po'," he says, jerking his head strangely to the darkness.

"What?" she replies, and passes shaken and dilated and brilliant, consciously ignoring him, passes away among the others, among those who are safe.

There is food in the kitchen, great hunks of bread, sliced sausage that Maria has made, wine, and a little coffee. But only the quality come to eat. The peasants may not come in. There is eating and drinking in the little house, the guitars are silent. It is eleven o'clock.

Then there is singing, the strange bestial singing of these hills. Sometimes the guitars can play an accompaniment, but usually not. Then the men lift up their heads and send out the high, half-howling music, astounding. The words are in dialect. They argue among themselves for a moment: will the Signoria understand? They sing. The Signoria does not understand in the least. So with a strange, slightly malignant triumph, the men sing all the verses of their song, sitting round the walls of the little parlour. Their throats move, their faces have a slight mocking smile. The boy capers in the doorway like a faun, with glee, his straight black hair falling over his forehead. The elder brother sits straight and flushed, but even his eyes glitter with a kind of yellow light of laughter. Paolo also sits quiet, with the invisible smile on his face. Only Maria, large and active, prospering now, keeps collected, ready to order a shrill silence in the same way as she orders the peasants, violently, to keep their places.

The boy comes to me and says:

"Do you know, Signore, what they are singing?"

"No," I say

So he capers with furious glee. The men with the watchful eyes, all roused, sit round the wall and sing more distinctly:

> Si verrà la primavera
> Fiorann' le mandoline,
> Vienn' di basso le Trentine
> Coi'taliani far'l'amor

But the next verses are so improper that I pretend not to understand. The women, with wakened, dilated faces, are listening, listening hard, their two faces beautiful in their attention, as if listening to something magical, a long way off. And the men sitting round the wall sing more plainly, coming nearer to the correct Italian. The song comes loud and vibrating and maliciously from their reedy throats, it pene-trates everybody. The foreign women can understand the sound, they can feel the malicious, suggestive mockery. But they cannot catch the words. The smile becomes more dangerous on the faces of the men.

Then Maria Fiori sees that I have understood, and she cries, in her loud, overriding voice:

"Basta – basta."

The men get up, straighten their bodies with a curious, offering movement. The guitars and mandolines strike the vibrating strings. But the vague Northern reserve has come over the Englishwomen. They dance again, but without the fusion in the dance. They have had enough.

The musicians are thanked, they rise and go into the night. The men pass off in pairs. But the wood-cutter, whose name and whose nickname I could never hear, still hovered on the edge of the darkness.

Then Maria sent him also away, complaining that he was too wild, *proprio selvatico*, and only the "quality" remained, the well-to-do youths from below. There was a little more coffee, and a talking, a story of a man who had fallen over a declivity in a lonely part going home drunk in the evening, and had lain unfound for eighteen hours. Then a story of a donkey who had kicked a youth in the chest and killed him.

But the women were tired, they would go to bed. Still the two young men would not go away. We all went out to look at the night.

The stars were very bright overhead, the mountain opposite and the mountains behind us faintly outlined themselves on the sky. Below, the lake was a black gulf. A little wind blew cold from the Adige.

In the morning the visitors had gone. They had insisted on staying the night. They had eaten eight eggs each and much bread at one o'clock in the morning. Then they had gone to sleep, lying on the floor in the sitting-room.

In the early sunshine they had drunk coffee and gone down to the village on the lake. Maria was very pleased. She would have made a good deal of money. The young men were rich. Her cupidity seemed like her very blossom.

ON THE LAGO DI GARDA

IL DURO

T HE FIRST TIME I SAW IL DURO WAS ON A SUNNY day when there came up a party of pleasure-makers to San Gaudenzio. They were three women and three men. The women were in cotton frocks, one a large, dark, florid woman in pink, the other two rather insignificant. The men I scarcely noticed at first, except that two were young and one elderly.

They were a queer party, even on a feast day, coming up purely for pleasure, in the morning, strange, and slightly uncertain, advancing between the vines. They greeted Maria and Paolo in loud, coarse voices. There was something blowsy and uncertain and hesitating about the women in particular, which made one at once notice them.

Then a picnic was arranged for them out of doors, on the grass. They sat just in front of the house, under the olive tree, beyond the well. It should have been pretty, the women in their cotton frocks, and their friends, sitting with wine and food in the spring sunshine. But somehow it was not: it was hard and slightly ugly.

But since they were picnicking out of doors, we must do so too. We were at once envious. But Maria was a little unwilling, and then she set a table for us.

The strange party did not speak to us, they seemed slightly uneasy and angry at our presence. I asked Maria who they were. She lifted her shoulders, and, after a second's cold pause, said they were people from down below, and then, in her rather strident, shrill, slightly bitter, slightly derogatory voice, she added:

"They are not people for you, Signore. You don't know them."

She spoke slightly angrily and contemptuously of them, rather protectively of me. So that vaguely I gathered that they were not quite "respectable".

Only one man came into the house. He was very handsome, beautiful rather, a man of thirty-two or -three, with a clear golden skin, and perfectly turned face, something godlike. But the expression was strange. His hair was jet black and fine and smooth, glossy as a bird's wing, his brows were beautifully drawn, calm above his grey eyes, that had long dark lashes.

His eyes, however, had a sinister light in them, a pale, slightly repelling gleam, very much like a god's pale-gleaming eyes, with the same vivid pallor. And all his face had the slightly malignant, suffering look of a satyr. Yet he was very beautiful.

He walked quickly and surely, with his head rather down, passing from his desire to his object, absorbed, yet curiously indifferent, as if the transit were in a strange world, as if none of what he was doing were worth the while. Yet he did it for his own pleasure, and the light on his face, a pale, strange gleam through his clear skin, remained like a translucent smile, unchanging as time.

He seemed familiar with the household, he came and

fetched wine at his will. Maria was angry with him. She railed loudly and violently. He was unchanged, He went out with the wine to the party on the grass. Maria regarded them all with some hostility.

They drank a good deal out there in the sunshine. The women and the older man talked floridly. Il Duro crouched at the feast in his curious fashion – he had strangely flexible loins, upon which he seemed to crouch forward. But he was separate, like an animal that remains quite single, no matter where it is.

The party remained until about two o'clock. Then, slightly flushed, it moved on in a ragged group up to the village beyond. I do not know if they went to one of the inns of the stony village, or to the large strange house which belonged to the rich young grocer of the village below, a house kept only for feasts and riots, uninhabited for the most part. Maria would tell me nothing about them. Only the young well-to-do grocer, who had lived in Vienna, the Bertolotti, came later in the afternoon enquiring for the party.

And towards sunset I saw the elderly man of the group stumbling home very drunk down the path, after the two women, who had gone on in front. Then Paolo sent Giovanni to see the drunken one safely past the landslip, which was dangerous. Altogether it was an unsatisfactory business, very much like any other such party in any other country.

Then in the evening Il Duro came in. His name is Faustino, but everybody in the village has a nickname, which is almost invariably used. He came in and asked for supper. We had all eaten. So he ate a little food alone at the table, whilst we sat round the fire.

Afterwards we played "Up, Jenkins". That was the one game we played with the peasants, except that exciting one of theirs, which consists in shouting in rapid succession your guesses at the number of fingers rapidly spread out and shut into the hands again upon the table.

Il Duro joined in the game. And that was because he had been in America, and now was rich. He felt he could come near to the strange signori. But he was always inscrutable.

It was queer to look at the hands spread on the table: the Englishwomen, having rings on their soft fingers; the large fresh hands of the elder boy, and brown paws of the younger; Paolo's distorted great hard hands of a peasant; and the big, dark brown, animal, shapely hands of Faustino.

He had been in America first for two years and then for five years – seven years altogether – but he only spoke a very little English. He was always with Italians. He had served chiefly in a flag factory, and had had very little to do save to push a trolley with flags from the dyeing-room to the drying-room – I believe it was this.

Then he had come home from America with a fair amount of money, he had taken his uncle's garden, had inherited his uncle's little house, and he lived quite alone.

He was rich, Maria said, shouting in her strident voice. He at once disclaimed it, peasant-wise. But before the signori he

was glad also to appear rich. He was mean, that was more, Maria cried, half-teasing, half getting at him.

He attended to his garden, grew vegetables all the year round, lived in his little house, and in spring made good money as a vine-grafter: he was an expert vine-grafter.

After the boys had gone to bed he sat and talked to me. He was curiously attractive and curiously beautiful, but somehow like stone in his clear colouring and his clear-cut face. His temples, with the black hair, were distinct and fine as a work of art.

But always his eyes had this strange, half-diabolic, half-tortured pale gleam, like a goat's, and his mouth was shut almost uglily, his cheeks stern. His moustache was brown, his teeth strong and spaced. The women said it was a pity his moustache was brown.

"Peccato! – sa, per bellezza, i baffi neri – ah-h!"

Then a long-drawn exclamation of voluptuous appreciation.

"You live quite alone?" I said to him.

He did. And even when he had been ill he was alone. He had been ill two years before. His cheeks seemed to harden like marble and to become pale at the thought. He was afraid, like marble with fear.

"But why," I said, "why do you live alone? You are sad – è triste."

He looked at me with his queer, pale eyes. I felt a great static misery in him, something very strange.

"Triste!" he repeated, stiffening up, hostile. I could not understand.

"Vuol' dire che hai l'aria dolorosa," cried Maria, like a chorus interpreting. And there was always a sort of loud ring of challenge somewhere in her voice.

"Sad," I said in English.

"Sad!" he repeated, also in English. And he did not smile or change, only his face seemed to become more stone-like. And he only looked at me, into my eyes, with the long, pale, steady, inscrutable look of a goat, I can only repeat, something stone-like.

"Why," I said, "don't you marry? Man doesn't live alone."

"I don't marry," he said to me, in his emphatic, deliberate cold fashion, "because I've seen too much. Ho visto troppo."

"I don't understand," I said.

Yet I could feel that Paolo, sitting silent, like a monolith also, in the chimney opening, he understood: Maria also understood.

Il Duro looked again steadily into my eyes.

"Ho visto troppo," he repeated, and the words seemed engraved on stone. "I've seen too much."

"But you can marry," I said, "however much you have seen, if you have seen all the world."

He watched me steadily, like a strange creature looking at me.

"What woman?" he said to me.

"You can find a woman – there are plenty of women," I said.

"Not for me," he said. "I have known too many. I've known too much, I can marry nobody."

"Do you dislike women?" I said.

"No – quite otherwise. I don't think ill of them."

"Then why can't you marry? Why must you live alone?"

"Why live with a woman?" he said to me, and he looked mockingly. "Which woman is it to be?"

"You can find her," I said. "There are many women."

Again he shook his head in the stony, final fashion.

"Not for me. I have known too much."

"But does that prevent you from marrying?"

He looked at me steadily, finally. And I could see it was impossible for us to understand each other, or for me to understand him. I could not understand the strange white gleam of his eyes, where it came from.

Also I knew he liked me very much, almost loved me, which again was strange and puzzling. It was as if he were a fairy, a faun, and had no soul. But he gave me a feeling of vivid sadness that gleamed like phosphorescence. He himself was not sad. There was a completeness about him, about the pallid otherworld he inhabited, which excluded sadness. It was too complete, to final, too defined. There was no yearning, no vague merging off into mistiness. . . . He was as clear and fine as semi-transparent rock, as a substance in moonlight. He seemed like a crystal that has achieved its final shape and has nothing more to achieve.

That night he slept on the floor of the sitting-room. In the morning he was gone. But a week after he came again, to graft the vines.

All the morning and the afternoon he was among the vines, crouching before them, cutting them back with his sharp, bright knife, amazingly swift and sure, like a god. It filled me with a sort of panic to see him crouched flexibly, like some strange animal god, doubled on his haunches, before the young vines, and swiftly, vividly, without thought, cut, cut, cut at the young budding shoots, which fell unheeded on to the earth. Then again he strode with his curious half-goatlike movement across the garden, to prepare the lime.

He mixed the messy stuff, cow-dung and lime and water and earth, carefully with his hands, as if he understood that too. He was not a worker. He was a creature in intimate communion with the sensible world, knowing purely by touch the limey mess he mixed amongst, knowing as if by relation between that soft matter and the matter of himself.

Then again he strode over the earth, a gleaming piece of earth himself, moving to the young vines. Quickly, with a few

clean cuts of the knife, he prepared the new shoot, which he had picked out of a handful which lay beside him on the ground; he went finely to the quick of the plant, inserted the graft, then bound it up, fast, hard.

It was like God grafting the life of man upon the body of the earth, intimately conjuring with his own flesh.

All the while Paolo stood by, somehow excluded from the mystery, talking to me, to Faustino. And Il Duro answered easily, as if his mind were disengaged. It was his senses that were absorbed in the sensible life of the plant, and the lime and the cow-dung he handled.

Watching him, watching his absorbed, bestial, and yet godlike crouching before the plant, as if he were the god of lower life, I somehow understood his isolation, why he did not marry. Pan and the ministers of Pan do not marry, the sylvan gods. They are single and isolated in their being.

It is in the spirit that marriage takes place. In the flesh there is connection, but only in the spirit is there a new thing created out of two different antithetic things. In the body I am conjoined with the woman. But in the spirit my conjunction with her creates a third thing, an absolute, a Word, which is neither me nor her, nor of me nor of her, but which is absolute.

And Faustino had none of this spirit. In him sensation itself was absolute – not spiritual consummation, but physical sensation. So he could not marry, it was not for him. He belonged to the god Pan, to the absolute of the senses.

All the while his beauty, so perfect and so defined, fascinated me, a strange static perfection about him. But his movements, whilst they fascinated, also repelled. I can always see him crouched before the vines on his haunches, his haunches doubled together in a complete animal unconsciousness, his face seeming in its strange golden pallor and its hardness of line, with the gleaming black of the fine hair on the brow and temples, like something reflective, like the

reflecting surface of a stone that gleams out of the depths of night. It was like darkness revealed in its steady, unchanging pallor.

Again he stayed through the evening, having quarrelled once more with the Maria about money. He quarrelled violently, yet coldly. There was something terrifying in it. And as soon as the matter of dispute was settled, all trace of interest or feeling vanished from him.

Yet he liked, above all things, to be near the English signori. They seemed to exercise a sort of magnetic attraction over him. It was something of the purely physical world, as a magnetised needle swings towards soft iron. He was quite helpless in the relation. Only by mechanical attraction he gravitated into line with us.

But there was nothing between us except our complete difference. It was like night and day flowing together.

ON THE
LAGO DI GARDA
JOHN

ESIDES IL DURO, WE FOUND ANOTHER ITALIAN who could speak English, this time quite well. We had walked about four or five miles up the lake, getting higher and higher. Then quite suddenly, on the shoulder of a bluff far up, we came on a village, icy cold, and as if forgotten.

We went into the inn to drink something hot. The fire of olive sticks was burning in the open chimney, one or two men were talking at a table, a young woman with a baby stood by the fire watching something boil in a large pot. Another woman was seen in the house-place beyond.

In the chimney-seats sat a young mule-driver, who had left his two mules at the door of the inn, and opposite him an elderly stout man. They got down and offered us the seats of honour, which we accepted with due courtesy.

The chimneys are like the wide, open chimney-places of old English cottages, but the hearth is raised about a foot and a half or two feet from the floor, so that the fire is almost level with the hands; and those who sit in the chimney-seats are raised above the audience in the room, something like two gods flanking the fire, looking out of the cave of ruddy darkness into the open, lower world of the room.

We asked for coffee with milk and rum. The stout landlord took a seat near us below. The comely young woman with the baby took the tin coffee-pot that stood among the grey ashes, put in fresh coffee among the old bottoms, filled it with water, then pushed it more into the fire.

The landlord turned to us with the usual naïve, curious deference, and the usual question:

"You are Germans?"

"English."

"Ah – Inglesi."

Then there is a new note of cordiality – or so I always imagine – and the rather rough, cattle-like men who are sitting with their wine round the table look up more amicably. They do not like being intruded upon. Only the landlord is always affable.

"I have a son who speaks English," he says: he is a handsome, courtly old man, of the Falstaff sort.

"Oh!"

"He has been in America."

"And where is he now?"

"He is at home. O – Nicoletta, where is the Giovann'?"

The comely young woman with the baby came in.

"He is with the band," she said.

The old landlord looked at her with pride.

"This is my daughter-in-law," he said.

She smiled readily to the Signora.

"And the baby?" we asked.

"Mio figlio," cried the young woman, in the strong, penetrating voice of these women. And she came forward to show the child to the Signora.

It was a bonny baby: the whole company was united in adoration and service of the bambino. There was a moment

of suspension, when religious submission seemed to come over the inn-room.

Then the Signora began to talk, and it broke upon the Italian child-reverence.

"What is he called?"

"Oscare," came the ringing note of pride. And the mother talked to the baby in dialect. All, men and women alike, felt themselves glorified by the presence of the child.

At last the coffee in the tin coffee-pot was boiling and frothing out of spout and lid. The milk in the little copper pan was also hot, among the ashes. So we had our drink at last.

The landlord was anxious for us to see Giovanni, his son. There was a village band performing up the street, in front of the house of a colonel who had come home wounded from Tripoli. Everybody in the village was wildly proud about the colonel and about the brass band, the music of which was execrable.

We just looked into the street. The band of uncouth fellows was playing the same tune over and over again before a desolate, newish house. A crowd of desolate, forgotten villagers stood around, in the cold upper air. It seemed altogether that the place was forgotten by God and man.

But the landlord, burly, courteous, handsome, pointed out with a flourish the Giovanni, standing in the band playing a cornet. The band itself consisted only of five men, rather like beggars in the street. But Giovanni was the strangest! He was tall and thin and somewhat German-looking, wearing shabby American clothes and a very high double collar and a small American crush hat. He looked entirely like a ne'er-do-well who plays a violin in the street, dressed in the most down-at-heel, sordid respectability.

"That is he – you see, Signore – the young one under the balcony."

The father spoke with love and pride, and the father was a gentleman, like Falstaff, a pure gentleman. The daughter-in-law also peered out to look at Il Giovann', who was evidently a figure of repute, in his sordid, degenerate American respectability. Meanwhile, this figure of repute blew himself red in the face, producing staccato strains on his cornet. And the crowd stood desolate and forsaken in the cold, upper afternoon.

Then there was a sudden rugged "Evviva, Evviva!" from the people, the band stopped playing, somebody valiantly broke into a line of the song:

> Tripoli, sarà italiana,
> Sarà italiana al rombo del cannon.

The colonel had appeared on the balcony, a smallish man, very yellow in the face, with grizzled black hair and very shabby legs. They all seemed so sordidly, hopelessly shabby.

He suddenly began to speak, leaning forward, hot and feverish and yellow, upon the iron rail of the balcony. There was something hot and marshy and sick about him, slightly repulsive, less than human. He told his fellow-villagers how he loved them, how, when he lay uncovered on the sands of Tripoli, week after week, he had known they were watching him from the Alpine height of the village, he could feel that where he was they were all looking. When the Arabs came rushing like things gone mad, and he had received his wound, he had known that in his own village, among his own dear ones, there was recovery. Love would heal the wounds, the home country was a lover who would heal all her sons' wounds with love.

Among the grey desolate crowd were sharp, rending "Bravos!" – the people were in tears – the landlord at my side was repeating softly, abstractedly: "Caro – caro – Ettore, caro colonello – " and when it was finished, and the little colonel with shabby, humiliated legs was gone in, he turned to me and said, with challenge that almost frightened me:

"Un brav' uomo."

"Bravissimo," I said.

Then we, too, went indoors.

It was all, somehow, grey and hopeless and acrid, unendurable.

The colonel, poor devil – we knew him afterwards – is now dead. It is strange that he is dead. There is something repulsive to me in the thought of his lying dead: such a humiliating, somehow degraded corpse. Death has no beauty in Italy, unless it be violent. The death of man or woman through sickness is an occasion of horror, repulsive. They belong entirely to life, they are so limited to life, these people.

Soon the Giovanni came home, and took his cornet upstairs. Then he came to see us. He was an ingenuous youth, sordidly shabby and dirty. His fair hair was long and uneven, his very high starched collar made one aware that his neck and his ears were not clean, his American crimson tie was ugly, his clothes looked as if they had been kicking about on the floor for a year.

Yet his blue eyes were warm and his manner and speech very gentle.

"You will speak English with us," I said.

"Oh," he said, smiling and shaking his head, "I could speak English very well. But it is two years that I don't speak it now, over two years now, so I don't speak it."

"But you speak it very well."

"No. It is two years that I have not spoke, not a word – so, you see, I have – "

"You have forgotten it? No, you haven't. It will quickly come back."

"If I hear it – when I go to America – then I shall – I shall"

"You will soon pick it up."

"Yes – I shall pick it up."

The landlord, who had been watching with pride, now went away. The wife also went away, and we were left with the shy, gentle, dirty, and frowsily-dressed Giovanni.

He laughed in his sensitive, quick fashion.

"The women in America, when they came into the store, they said, 'Where is John, where is John?' Yes, they liked me."

And he laughed again, glancing with vague, warm blue eyes, very shy, very coiled upon himself with sensitiveness.

He had managed a store in America, in a smallish town. I glanced at his reddish, smooth, rather knuckly hands, and thin wrists in the frayed cuff. They were real shopman's hands.

The landlord brought some special feast-day cake, so overjoyed he was to have his Giovanni speaking English with the Signoria.

When we went away, we asked "John" to come down to our villa to see us. We scarcely expected him to turn up.

Yet one morning he appeared, at about half-past nine, just as we were finishing breakfast. It was sunny and warm and beautiful, so we asked him please to come with us picnicking.

He was a queer shoot, again, in his unkempt longish hair and slovenly clothes, a sort of very vulgar down-at-heel American in appearance. And he was transported with shyness. Yet ours was the world he had chosen as his own, so he took his place bravely and simply, a hanger-on.

We climbed up the water-course in the mountain-side, up to a smooth little lawn under the olive trees, where daisies were flowering and gladioli were in bud. It was a tiny little lawn of grass in a level crevice, and sitting there we had the world below us – the lake, the distant island, the far-off low Verona shore.

Then "John" began to talk, and he talked continuously, like a foreigner, not saying the things he would have said in Italian, but following the suggestion and scope of his limited English.

In the first place, he loved his father – it was "my father, my father" always. His father had a little shop as well as the inn in the village above. So John had had some education.

He had been sent to Brescia and then to Verona to school, and there had taken his examinations to become a civil engineer. He was clever, and could pass his examinations. But he never finished his course. His mother died, and his father, disconsolate, had wanted him at home. Then he had gone back, when he was sixteen or seventeen, to the village beyond the lake, to be with his father and look after the shop.

"But didn't you mind giving up all your work?" I said.

He did not quite understand.

"My father wanted me to come back," he said.

It was evident that Giovanni had had no definite conception of what he was doing or what he wanted to do. His father, wishing to make a gentleman of him, had sent him to school in Verona. By accident he had been moved on into the engineering course. When it all fizzled to an end, and he returned half-baked to the remote, desolate village of the mountain-side, he was not disappointed or chagrined. He had never conceived of a coherent purposive life. Either one stayed in the village, like a lodged stone, or one made random excursions into the world, across the world. It was all aimless and purposeless.

So he had stayed a while with his father, then he had gone, just as aimlessly, with a party of men who were emigrating to America. He had taken some money, had drifted about, living in the most comfortless, wretched fashion, then he had found a place somewhere in Pennsylvania, in a dry goods store. This was when he was seventeen or eighteen years old.

All this seemed to have happened to him without his being very much affected, at least consciously. His nature was simple and self-complete. Yet not so self-complete as that of Il Duro or Paolo. They had passed through the foreign world and been quite untouched. Their souls were static, it was the world that had flowed unstable by.

But John was more sensitive, he had come more into contact with his new surroundings. He had attended night classes almost every evening, and had been taught English like a child. He had loved the American free school, the teachers, the work.

But he had suffered very much in America. With his curious, over-sensitive, wincing laugh, he told us how the boys had followed him and jeered at him, calling after him, "You damn Dago, you damn Dago." They had stopped him and his friend in the street and taken away their hats, and spat into them. So that at last he had gone mad. They were youths and men who always tortured him, using bad language which startled us very much as he repeated it, there on the little lawn under the olive trees, above the perfect lake: English obscenities and abuse so coarse and startling that we bit our lips, shocked almost into laughter, whilst John, simple and natural, and somehow, for all his long hair and dirty appearance, flower-like in soul, repeated to us these things which may never be repeated in decent company.

"Oh," he said, "at last, I get mad. When they come one day, shouting, 'You damn Dago, dirty dog,' and will take my hat again, oh, I get mad, and I would kill them. I would kill them, I am so mad. I run to them, and throw one to the floor, and I tread on him while I go upon another, the biggest. Though they hit me and kick me all over, I feel nothing, I am mad. I throw the biggest to the floor, a man; he is older than I am, and I hit him so hard I would kill him. When the others see it they are afraid, they throw stones and hit me on the face. But I don't feel it – I don't know nothing. I hit the man on the floor, I almost kill him. I forget everything except I will kill him – "

"But you didn't?"

"No – I don't know – " and he laughed his queer, shaken laugh. "The other man that was with me, my friend, he came to me and we went away. Oh, I was mad, I was competely mad. I would have killed them."

He was trembling slightly, and his eyes were dilated with a strange greyish-blue fire that was very painful and elemental. He looked beside himself. But he was by no means mad.

We were shaken by the vivid, lambent excitement of the youth, we wished him to forget. We were shocked, too, in our souls to see the pure elemental flame shaken out of his gentle, sensitive nature. By his slight, crinkled laugh we could see how much he had suffered. He had gone out and faced the world, and he had kept his place, stranger and Dago though he was.

"They never came after me no more, not all the while I was there."

Then he said he became the foreman in the store – at first he was only assistant. It was the best store in the town, and many English ladies came, and some Germans. He liked the English ladies very much: they always wanted him to be in the store. He wore white clothes there, and they would say:

"You look very nice in the white coat, John"; or else:

"Let John come, he can find it"; or else they said:

"John speaks like a born American."

This pleased him very much.

In the end, he said, he earned a hundred dollars a month. He lived with the extraordinary frugality of the Italians and had quite a lot of money.

He was not like Il Duro. Faustino had lived in a state of miserliness almost in America, but then he had had his debauches of shows and wine and carousals. John went chiefly to the schools, in one of which he was even asked to teach Italian. His knowledge of his own language was re-markable and most unusual!

"But what," I asked, "brought you back?"

"It was my father. You see, if I did not come to have my military service, I must stay till I am forty. So I think perhaps my father will be dead, I shall never see him. So I came."

He had come home when he was twenty to fulfil his military duties. At home he had married. He was very fond of his wife, but he had no conception of love in the old sense. His

wife was like the past, to which he was wedded. Out of her he begot his child, as out of the past. But the future was all beyond her, apart from her. He was going away again, now, to America. He had been some nine months at home after his military service was over. He had no more to do. Now he was leaving his wife and child and his father to go to America.

"But why," I said, "why? You are not poor, you can manage the shop in your village."

"Yes," he said. "But I will go to America. Perhaps I shall go into the store again, the same."

"But is it not just the same as managing the shop at home?"

"No – no – it is quite different."

Then he told us how he bought goods in Brescia and in Salò for the shop at home, how he had rigged up a funicular with the assistance of the village, an overhead wire by which you could haul the goods up the face of the cliffs right high up, to within a mile of the village. He was very proud of this. And sometimes he himself went down the funicular to the water's edge, to the boat, when he was in a hurry. This also pleased him.

But he was going to Brescia this day to see about going again to America. Perhaps in another month he would be gone.

It was a great puzzle to me why he would go. He could not say himself. He would stay four or five years, then he would come home again to see his father – and his wife and child.

There was a strange, almost frightening destiny upon him, which seemed to take him away, always away from home, from the past, to that great, raw America. He seemed scarcely like a person with individual choice, more like a creature under the influence of fate which was disintegrating the old life and precipitating him, a fragment inconclusive, into the new chaos.

He submitted to it all with a perfect unquestioning simplicity, never even knowing that he suffered, that he must suffer disintegration from the old life. He was moved entirely from within, he never questioned his inevitable impulse.

"They say to me, 'Don't go – don't go' –" he shook his head. "But I say I will go."

And at that it was finished.

So we saw him off at the little quay, going down the lake. He would return at evening, and be pulled up in his funicular basket. And in a month's time he would be standing on the same lake steamer going to America.

Nothing was more painful than to see him standing there in his degraded, sordid American clothes, on the deck of the steamer, waving us good-bye, belonging in his final desire to our world, the world of consciousness and deliberate action. With his candid, open, unquestioning face, he seemed like a prisoner being conveyed from one form of life to another, or like a soul in trajectory, that has not yet found a resting-place.

What were wife and child to him? – they were the last steps of the past. His father was the continent behind him; his wife and child the foreshore of the past; but his face was set outwards, away from it all – whither, neither he nor anybody knew, but he called it America.

ITALIANS
IN EXILE

W HEN I WAS IN CONSTANCE THE WEATHER WAS misty and enervating and depressing, it was no pleasure to travel on the big flat desolate lake.

When I went from Constance, it was on a small steamer down the Rhine to Schaffhausen. That was beautiful. Still, the mist hung over the waters, over the wide shallows of the river, and the sun, coming through the morning, made lovely yellow lights beneath the bluish haze, so that it seemed like the beginning of the world. And there was a hawk in the upper air fighting with two crows, or two rooks. Ever they rose higher and higher, the crow flickering above the attacking hawk, the fight going on like some strange symbol in the sky, the Germans on deck watching with pleasure.

Then we passed out of sight between wooded banks and under bridges where quaint villages of old romance piled their red and coloured pointed roofs beside the water, very still, remote, lost in the vagueness of the past. It could not be that they were real. Even when the boat put in to shore, and the customs officials came to look, the village remained remote in the romantic past of High Germany, the Germany of fairy tales and minstrels and craftsmen. The poignancy of the past was almost unbearable, floating there in colour upon the haze of the river.

We went by some swimmers, whose white shadowy bodies trembled near the side of the steamer under water.

One man with a round, fair head lifted his face and one arm from the water and shouted a greeting to us, as if he were a Niebelung, saluting with bright arm lifted from the water, his face laughing, the fair moustache hanging over his mouth. Then his white body swirled in the water, and he was gone, swimming with the side stroke.

Schaffhausen the town, half old and bygone, half modern, with breweries and industries, that is not very real. Schaffhausen Falls, with their factory in the midst and their hotel at the bottom, and the general cinematograph effect, they are ugly.

It was afternoon when I set out to walk from the Falls to Italy, across Switzerland. I remember the big, fat, rather gloomy fields of this part of Baden, damp and unliving. I remember I found some apples under a tree in a field near a railway embankment, then some mushrooms, and I ate both. Then I came on to a long, desolate high-road, with dreary, withered trees on either side, and flanked by great fields where groups of men and women were working. They looked at me as I went by down the long, long road, alone and exposed and out of the world.

I remember nobody came at the border village to examine my pack, I passed through unchallenged. All was quiet and lifeless and hopeless, with big stretches of heavy land.

Till sunset came, very red and purple, and suddenly, from the heavy spacious open land I dropped sharply into the

Rhine valley again, suddenly, as if into another glamorous world.

There was the river rushing along between its high, mysterious, romantic banks, which were high as hills, and covered with vine. And there was the village of tall, quaint houses flickering its lights on to the deep-flowing river, and quite silent, save for the rushing of water.

There was a fine covered bridge, very dark. I went to the middle and looked through the opening at the dark water below, at the façade of square lights, the tall village-front towering remote and silent above the river. The hill rose on either side the flood; down here was a small, forgotten, wonderful world that belonged to the date of isolated village communities and wandering minstrels.

So I went back to the inn of "The Golden Stag", and, climbing some steps, I made a loud noise. A woman came, and I asked for food. She led me through a room where were enormous barrels, ten feet in diameter, lying fatly on their sides;

then through a large stone-clean kitchen, with bright pans, ancient as the Meistersinger; then up some steps and into the long guest-room, where a few tables were laid for supper.

A few people were eating. I asked for Abendessen, and sat by the window looking at the darkness of the river below, the covered bridge, the dark hill opposite, crested with its few lights.

Then I ate a very large quantity of knoedel soup and bread, and drank beer, and was very sleepy. Only one or two village men came in, and these soon went again; the place was dead still. Only at a long table on the opposite side of the room were seated seven or eight men, ragged, disreputable, some impudent – another came in late; the landlady gave them all thick soup with dumplings and bread and meat, serving them in a sort of brief disapprobation. They sat at the long table, eight or nine tramps and beggars and wanderers out of work, and they ate with a sort of cheerful callousness and brutality for the most part, and as if ravenously, looking round and grinning sometimes, subdued, cowed, like prisoners, and yet impudent. At the end one shouted to know where he was to sleep. The landlady called to the young serving-woman, and in a classic German severity of disapprobation they were led up the stone stairs to their room. They tramped off in threes and twos, making a bad, mean, humiliated exit. It was not yet eight o'clock. The landlady sat talking to one bearded man, staid and severe, whilst, with her work on the table, she sewed steadily.

As the beggars and wanderers went slinking out of the room, some called impudently, cheerfully:

"Nacht, Frau Wirtin – G'Nacht, Wirtin – 'te Nacht, Frau," to all of which the hostess answered a stereotyped "Gute Nacht," never turning her head from her sewing, or indicating by the faintest movement that she was addressing the men who were filing raggedly to the doorway.

So the room was empty, save for the landlady and her sewing, the staid, elderly villager to whom she was talking in the unbeautiful dialect, and the young serving-woman who was clearing away the plates and basins of the tramps and beggars.

Then the villager also went.

"Gute Nacht, Frau Seidl," to the landlady; "Gute Nacht," at random, to me.

So I looked at the newspaper. Then I asked the landlady for a cigarette, not knowing how else to begin. So she came to my table, and we talked.

It pleased me to take upon myself a sort of romantic, wandering character; she said my German was "schön"; a little goes a long way.

So I asked her who were the men who had sat at the long table. She became rather stiff and curt.

"They are the men looking for work," she said, as if the subject were disagreeable.

"But why do they come here, so many?" I asked.

Then she told me that they were going out of the country: this was almost the last village of the border: that the relieving officer in each village was empowered to give to every vagrant a ticket entitling the holder to an evening meal, bed, and bread in the morning, at a certain inn. This was the inn for the vagrants coming to this village. The landlady received fourpence per head, I believe it was, for each of these wanderers.

"Little enough," I said.

"Nothing," she replied.

She did not like the subject at all. Only her respect for me made her answer.

"Bettler, Lumpen, und Taugenichtse!" I said cheerfully.

"And men who are out of work, and are going back to their own parish," she said stiffly.

So we talked a little, and I too went to bed.

"Gute Nacht, Frau Wirtin."

"Gute Nacht, mein Herr."

So I went up more and more stone stairs, attended by the

young woman. It was a great, lofty, old deserted house, with many drab doors.

At last, in the distant topmost floor, I had my bedroom, with two beds and bare floor and scant furniture. I looked down at the river far below, at the covered bridge, at the far lights on the hill above, opposite. Strange to be here in this lost, forgotten place, sleeping under the roof with tramps and beggars. I debated whether they would steal my boots if I put them out. But I risked it. The door-latch made a loud noise on the deserted landing, everywhere felt abandoned, forgotten. I wondered where the eight tramps and beggars were asleep. There was no way of securing the door. But somehow I felt that, if I were destined to be robbed or murdered, it would not be by tramps and beggars. So I blew out the candle and lay under the big feather bed, listening to the running and whispering of the mediaeval Rhine.

And when I waked up again it was sunny, it was morning on the hill opposite, though the river deep below ran in shadow.

The tramps and beggars were all gone: they must be cleared out by seven o'clock in the morning. So I had the inn to myself, I, and the landlady, and the serving-woman. Everywhere was very clean, full of the German morning energy and brightness, which is so different from the Latin morning. The Italians are dead and torpid first thing, the Germans are energetic and cheerful.

It was cheerful in the sunny morning, looking down on the swift river, the covered, picturesque bridge, the bank and the hill opposite. Then down the curving road of the facing hill the Swiss cavalry came riding, men in blue uniforms. I went out to watch them. They came thundering romantically through the dark cavern of the roofed-in bridge, and they dismounted at the entrance to the village. There was a fresh morning-cheerful newness everywhere, in the arrival of the troops, in the welcome of the villagers.

The Swiss do not look very military, neither in accoutrement nor in bearing. This little squad of cavalry seemed more like a party of common men riding out on some business of their own than like an army. They were very republican and very free. The officer who commanded them was one of themselves, his authority was by consent.

It was all very pleasant and genuine; there was a sense of ease and peacefulness, quite different from the mechanical, slightly sullen manoeuvring of the Germans.

The village baker and his assistant came hot and floury from the bakehouse, bearing between them a great basket of fresh bread. The cavalry were all dismounted by the bridge-head, eating and drinking like business men. Villagers came to greet their friends: one soldier kissed his father, who came wearing a leathern apron. The school bell tang-tang-tanged from above, school children merged timidly through the grouped horses, up the narrow street, passing unwillingly with their books. The river ran swiftly, the soldiers, very haphazard and slack in uniform, real shack-bags, chewed their

bread in large mouthfuls; the young lieutenant, who seemed to be an officer only by consent of the men, stood apart by the bridge-head, gravely. They were all serious and self-contented, very unglamorous. It was like a business excursion on horseback, harmless and uninspiring. The uniforms were almost ludicrous, so ill-fitting and casual.

So I shouldered by own pack and set off, through the bridge over the Rhine, and up the hill opposite.

There is something very dead about this country. I remember I picked apples from the grass by the roadside, and some were very sweet. But for the rest, there was mile after mile of dead, uninspired country – uninspired, so neutral and ordinary that it was almost destructive.

One gets this feeling always in Switzerland, except high up: this feeling of average, of utter soulless ordinariness, something intolerable. Mile after mile, to Zurich, it was just the same. It was just the same in the tram-car going into Zurich; it was just the same in the town, in the shops, in the restaurant. All was the utmost level of ordinariness and well-being, but so ordinary that it was like a blight. All the picturesqueness of the town is as nothing, it is like a most ordinary, average, usual person in an old costume. The place was soul-killing.

So after two hours' rest, eating in a restaurant, wandering by the quay and through the market, and sitting on a seat by the lake, I found a steamer that would take me away. That is how I always feel in Switzerland: the only possible living sensation is the sensation of relief in going away, always going away. The horrible average ordinariness of it all, something utterly without flower or soul or transcendence, the horrible vigorous ordinariness, is too much.

So I went on a steamer down the long lake, surrounded by low grey hills. It was Saturday afternoon. A thin rain came on. I thought I would rather be in fiery Hell than in this dead level of average life.

I landed somewhere on the right bank, about three-quarters of the way down the lake. It was almost dark. Yet I must walk away. I climbed a long hill from the lake, came to the crest, looked down the darkness of the valley, and descended into the deep gloom, down into a soulless village.

But it was eight o'clock, and I had had enough. One might as well sleep. I found the "Gasthaus zur Post".

It was a small, very rough inn, having only one common room, with bare tables, and a short, stout, grim, rather surly landlady, and a landlord whose hair stood up on end, and who was trembling on the edge of delirium tremens.

They could only give me boiled ham: so I ate boiled ham and drank beer, and tried to digest the utter cold materialism of Switzerland.

As I sat with my back to the wall, staring blankly at the trembling landlord, who was ready at any moment to foam at the mouth, and at the dour landlady, who was quite capable of keeping him in order, there came in one of those dark, showy Italian girls with a man. She wore a blouse and skirt, and no hat. Her hair was perfectly dressed. It was really Italy. The man was soft, dark, he would get stout later, *trapu*, he would have somewhat the figure of Caruso. But as yet he was soft, sensuous, young, handsome.

They sat at the long side-table with their beer, and created another country at once within the room. Another Italian came, fair and fat and slow, one from the Venetian province; then another, a little thin young man, who might have been a Swiss save for his vivid movement.

This last was the first to speak to the Germans. The others had just said "Bier." But the little new-comer entered into a conversation with the landlady.

At last there were six Italians sitting talking loudly and warmly at the side-table. The slow, cold German-Swiss at the other tables looked at them occasionally. The landlord, with his crazed, stretched eyes, glared at them with hatred. But they fetched their beer from the bar with easy familiarity, and sat at their table, creating a bonfire of life in the callousness of the inn.

At last they finished their beer and trooped off down the passage. The room was painfully empty. I did not know what to do.

Then I heard the landlord yelling and screeching and snarling from the kitchen at the back, for all the world like a mad dog. But the Swiss Saturday evening customers at the other tables smoked on and talked in their ugly dialect, without trouble. Then the landlady came in, and soon after the landlord, he collarless, with his waistcoat unbuttoned, showing his loose throat, and accentuating his round pot-belly. His limbs were thin and feverish, the skin of his face hung loose, his eyes were glaring, his hands trembled. Then he sat down to talk to a crony. His terrible appearance was a fiasco; nobody heeded him at all, only the landlady was surly.

From the back came loud noises of pleasure and excitement and banging about. When the room door was opened I could see down the dark passage opposite another lighted door. Then the fat, fair Italian came in for more beer.

"What is all the noise?" I asked the landlady at last.

"It is the Italians," she said.

"What are they doing?"

"They are doing a play."

"Where?"

She jerked her head: "In the room at the back."

"Can I go and look at them?"

"I should think so."

The landlord glaringly watched me go out. I went down the stone passage and found a great, half-lighted room that might be used to hold meetings, with forms piled at the side. At one end was a raised platform or stage. And on this stage was a table and a lamp, and the Italians grouped round the light, gesticulating and laughing. Their beer mugs were on the table and on the floor of the stage; the little sharp youth was intently looking over some papers, the others were bending over the table with him.

They looked up as I entered from the distance, looked at me in the distant twilight of the dusky room, as if I were an intruder, as if I should go away when I had seen them. But I said in German:

"May I look?"

They were still unwilling to see or to hear me.

"What do you say?" the small one asked in reply.

The others stood and watched, slightly at bay, like suspicious animals.

"If I might come and look," I said in German; then, feeling very uncomfortable, in Italian: "You are doing a drama, the landlady told me."

The big empty room was behind me, dark, the little company of Italians stood above me in the light of the lamp which was on the table. They all watched with unseeing, unwilling looks: I was merely an intrusion.

"We are only learning it," said the small youth.

They wanted me to go away. But I wanted to stay.

"May I listen?" I said. "I don't want to stay in there." And I indicated, with a movement of the head, the inn-room beyond.

"Yes," said the young intelligent man. "But we are only reading our parts."

They had all become more friendly to me, they accepted me.

"You are a German?" asked one youth.

"No – English."

"English? But do you live in Switzerland?"

"No – I am walking to Italy."

"On foot?"

They looked with wakened eyes.

"Yes."

So I told them about my journey. They were puzzled. They did not quite understand why I wanted to walk. But they were delighted with the idea of going to Lugano and Como and then to Milan.

"Where do you come from?" I asked them.

They were all from the villages between Verona and Venice. They had seen the Garda. I told them of my living there.

"Those peasants of the mountains," they said at once, "they are people of little education. Rather wild folk."

And they spoke with good-humoured contempt.

I thought of Paolo, and Il Duro, and the Signor Pietro, our padrone, and I resented these factory-hands for criticising them.

So I sat on the edge of the stage whilst they rehearsed their parts. The little thin intelligent fellow, Giuseppino, was the leader. The others read their parts in the laborious, disjointed fashion of the peasant, who can only see one word at a time, and has then to put the words together, afterwards, to make sense. The play was an amateur melodrama, printed in little penny booklets, for carnival production. This was only the second reading they had given it, and the handsome, dark fellow, who was roused and displaying himself before the girl, a

hard, erect piece of callousness, laughed and flushed and stumbled, and understood nothing till it was transferred into him direct through Giuseppino. The fat, fair, slow man was more conscientious. He laboured through his part. The other two men were in the background more or less.

The most confidential was the fat, fair, slow man, who was called Alberto. His part was not very important, so he could sit by me and talk to me.

He said they were all workers in the factory – silk, I think it was – in the village. They were a whole colony of Italians, thirty or more families. They had all come at different times.

Giuseppino had been longest in the village. He had come when he was eleven, with his parents, and had attended the Swiss school. So he spoke perfect German. He was a clever man, was married, and had two children.

He himself, Alberto, had been seven years in the valley; the girl, la Maddelena, had been here ten years; the dark man, Alfredo, who was flushed with excitement of her, had been in the village about nine years – he alone of all the men was not married.

The others had all married Italian wives, and they lived in the great dwelling whose windows shone yellow by the rattling factory. They lived entirely among themselves; none of them could speak German, more than a few words, except the Giuseppino, who was like a native here.

It was very strange being among these Italians exiled in Switzerland. Alfredo, the dark one, the unmarried, was in the old tradition. Yet even he was curiously subject to a new purpose, as if there were some greater new will that included him, sensuous, mindless as he was. He seemed to give his consent to something beyond himself. In this he was different from Il Duro, in that he had put himself under the control of the outside conception.

It was strange to watch them on the stage, the Italians all lambent, soft, warm, sensuous, yet moving subject round Giuseppino, who was always quiet, always ready, always impersonal. There was a look of purpose, almost of devotion on his face, that singled him out and made him seem the one stable, eternal being among them. They quarrelled, and he let them quarrel up to a certain point; then he called them back. He let them do as they liked so long as they adhered more or less to the central purpose, so long as they got on in some measure with the play.

All the while they were drinking beer and smoking cigarettes. The Alberto was barman: he went out continually with the glasses. The Maddelena had a small glass. In the lamplight of the stage the little party read and smoked and practised, exposed to the empty darkness of the big room. Queer and isolated it seemed, a tiny, pathetic magic-land far away from the barrenness of Switzerland. I could believe in the old fairytales where, when the rock was opened, a magic underworld was revealed.

The Alfredo, flushed, roused, handsome, but very soft and enveloping in his heat, laughed and threw himself into his pose, laughed foolishly, and then gave himself up to his part. The Alberto, slow and laborious, yet with a spark of vividness and natural intensity flashing through, replied and gesticulated; the Maddelena laid her head on the bosom of Alfredo, the other men started into action, and the play proceeded intently for half an hour.

Quick, vivid, and sharp, the little Giuseppino was always central. But he seemed almost invisible. When I think back, I can scarcely see him, I can only see the others, the lamplight on their faces and on their full gesticulating limbs. I can see the Maddelena, rather coarse and hard and repellent, declaiming her words in a loud, half-cynical voice, falling on the breast of the Alfredo, who was soft and sensuous, more like a female, flushing, with his mouth getting wet, his eyes moist, as he was roused. I can see the Alberto, slow, laboured, yet with a kind of pristine simplicity in all his movements, that touched his fat commonplaceness with beauty. Then there were the two other men, shy, inflam-

Lauterbrunnen.   Albert Goodwin

mable, unintelligent, with their sudden Italian rushes of hot feeling. All their faces are distinct in the lamplight, all their bodies are palpable and dramatic.

But the face of the Giuseppino is like a pale luminousness, a sort of gleam among all the ruddy glow, his body is evanescent, like a shadow. And his being seemed to cast its influence over all the others, except perhaps the woman, who was hard and resistant. The other men seemed all overcast, mitigated, in part transfigured by the will of the little leader. But they were very soft stuff, if inflammable.

The young woman of the inn, niece of the landlady, came down and called out across the room.

"We will go away from here now," said the Giuseppino to me. "They close at eleven. But we have another inn in the next parish that is open all night. Come with us and drink some wine."

"But," I said, "you would rather be alone."

No; they pressed me to go, they wanted me to go with them, they were eager, they wanted to entertain me. Alfredo, flushed, wet-mouthed, warm, protested I must drink wine, the real Italian red wine, from their own village at home. They would have no nay.

So I told the landlady. She said I must be back by twelve o'clock.

The night was very dark. Below the road the stream was rushing; there was a great factory on the other side of the water, making faint quivering lights of reflection, and one could see the working of machinery shadowy through the lighted windows. Near by was the tall tenement where the Italians lived.

We went on through the straggling, raw village, deep beside the stream, then over the small bridge, and up the steep hill down which I had come earlier in the evening.

So we arrived at the café. It was so different inside from the German inn, yet it was not like an Italian café either. It was brilliantly lighted, clean, new, and there were red-and-white cloths on the tables. The host was in the room, and his daughter, a beautiful red-haired girl.

Greetings were exchanged with the quick, intimate directness of Italy. But there was another note also, a faint echo of reserve, as though they reserved themselves from the outer world, making a special inner community.

Alfredo was hot: he took off his coat. We all sat freely at a long table, whilst the red-haired girl brought a quart of red wine. At other tables men were playing cards, with the odd Neapolitan cards. They too were talking Italian. It was a warm, ruddy bit of Italy within the cold darkness of Switzerland.

"When you come to Italy," they said to me, "salute it from us, salute the sun, and the earth, l' Italia."

So we drank in salute of Italy. They sent their greeting by me.

"You know in Italy there is the sun, the sun," said Alfredo to me, profoundly moved, wet-mouthed, tipsy.

I was reminded of Enrico Persevalli and his terrifying cry at the end of "*Ghosts*":

"Il sole, il sole!"

So we talked for a while of Italy. They had a pained tenderness for it, sad, reserved.

"Don't you want to go back?" I said, pressing them to tell me definitely. "Won't you go back some time?"

"Yes," they said, "we will go back."

But they spoke reservedly, without freedom. We talked about Italy, about songs, and Carnival; about the food, polenta, and salt. They laughed at my pretending to cut the slabs of polenta with a string: that rejoiced them all: it took them back to the Italian mezzo-giorno, the bells jangling in the campanile, the eating after the heavy work on the land.

But they laughed with the slight pain and contempt and fondness which every man feels towards his past, when he has struggled away from that past, from the conditions which made it.

They loved Italy passionately; but they would not go back. All their blood, all their senses were Italian, needed the Italian sky, the speech, the sensuous life. They could hardly live except through the senses. Their minds were not developed, mentally they were children, lovable, naïve, almost fragile children. But sensually they were men: sensually they were accomplished.

Yet a new tiny flower was struggling to open in them, the flower of a new spirit. The substratum of Italy has always been pagan, sensuous, the most potent symbol the sexual symbol. The child is really a non-Christian symbol: it is the symbol of man's triumph of eternal life in procreation. The worship of the Cross never really held good in Italy. The Christianity of Northern Europe has never had any place there.

And now, when Northern Europe is turning back on its own Christianity, denying it all, the Italians are struggling with might and main against the sensuous spirit which still dominates them. When Northern Europe, whether it hates Nietzsche or not, is crying out for the Dionysic ecstasy, practising on itself the Dionysic ecstasy, Southern Europe is breaking free from Dionysos, from the triumphal affirmation of life over death, immortality through procreation.

I could see these sons of Italy would never go back. Men like Paolo and Il Duro broke away only to return. The dominance of the old form was too strong for them. Call it love of country or love of the village, companilismo, or what not, it was the dominance of the old pagan form, the old affirmation of immortality through procreation, as opposed to the Christian affirmation of immortality through self-death and social love.

But "John" and these Italians in Switzerland were a generation younger, and they would not go back, at least not to the old Italy. Suffer as they might, and they did suffer, wincing in every nerve and fibre from the cold material insentience of the northern countries and of America, still they would endure this for the sake of something else they wanted. They would suffer a death in the flesh, as "John" had suffered in fighting the street crowd, as these men suffered year after year cramped in their black gloomy cold Swiss valley, working in the factory. But there would come a new spirit out of it.

Even Alfredo was submitted to the new process; though he belonged entirely by nature to the sort of Il Duro, he was purely sensuous and mindless. But under the influence of Giuseppino he was thrown down, as fallow to the new spirit that would come.

And then, when the others were all partially tipsy, the Giuseppino began to talk to me. In him was a steady flame burning, burning, burning, a flame of the mind, of the spirit, something new and clear, something that held even the soft, sensuous Alfredo in submission, besides all the others, who had some little development of mind.

"Sa signore," said the Giuseppino to me, quiet, almost invisible or inaudible, as it seemed, like a spirit addressing me, "l'uomo non ha patria – a man has no country. What has the Italian Government to do with us? What does a Government mean? It makes us work, it takes part of our wages away from us, it makes us soldiers – and what for? What is government for?"

"Have you been a soldier?" I interrupted him.

He had not, none of them had: that was why they could not really go back to Italy. Now this was out; this explained partly their curious reservation in speaking about their beloved country. They had forfeited parents as well as homeland.

"What does the Government do? It takes taxes; it has an army and police, and it makes roads. But we could do without an army, and we could be our own police, and we could make our own roads. What is this Government? Who wants it? Only those who are unjust, and want to have advantage over somebody else. It is an instrument of injustice and of wrong.

"Why should we have a Government? Here, in this village, there are thirty families of Italians. There is no government for them, no Italian Government. And we live together better than in Italy. We are richer and freer, we have no policemen, no poor laws. We help each other, and there are no poor.

"Why are these Governments always doing what we don't want them to do? We should not be fighting in the Cirenaica if we were all Italians. It is the Government that does it. They talk and talk and do things with us: but we don't want them."

The others, tipsy, sat round the table with the terrified gravity of children who are somehow responsible for things they do not understand. They stirred in their seats, turning aside, with gestures almost of pain, of imprisonment. Only Alfredo, laying his hand on mine, was laughing, loosely, floridly. He would upset all the Government with a jerk of his well-built shoulder, and then he would have a spree – such a spree. He laughed wetly to me.

The Giuseppino waited patiently during this tipsy confidence, but his pale clarity and beauty was something constant and star-like in comparison with the flushed, soft handsomeness of the other. He waited patiently, looking at me.

But I did not want him to go on: I did not want to answer. I could feel a new spirit in him, something strange and pure and slightly frightening. He wanted something which was beyond me. And my soul was somewhere in tears, crying helplessly like an infant in the night. I could not respond: I could not answer. He seemed to look at me, me, an Englishman, an educated man, for corroboration. But I could not corroborate him. I knew the purity and new struggling towards birth of a true star-like spirit. But I could not confirm him in his utterance: my soul could not respond. I did not believe in the perfectibility of man. I did not believe in infinite harmony among men. And this was his star, this belief.

It was nearly midnight. A Swiss came in and asked for beer. The Italians gathered round them a curious darkness of reserve. And then I must go.

They shook hands with me warmly, truthfully, putting a sort of implicit belief in me, as representative of some further knowledge. But there was a fixed, calm resolve over the face of the Giuseppino, a sort of steady faith, even in disappointment. He gave me a copy of a little Anarchist paper published in Geneva. *L'Anarchista*, I believe it was called. I glanced at it. It was in Italian, naïve, simple, rather rhetorical. So they were all Anarchists, these Italians.

I ran down the hill in the thick Swiss darkness to the little bridge, and along the uneven cobbled street. I did not want to think, I did not want to know. I wanted to arrest my activity, to keep it confined to the moment, to the adventure.

When I came to the flight of stone steps which led up to the door of the inn, at the side I saw in the darkness two figures. They said a low good-night and parted; the girl began to knock at the door, the man disappeared. It was the niece of the landlady parting from her lover.

We waited outside the locked door, at the top of the stone steps, in the darkness of midnight. The stream rustled below. Then came a shouting and an insane snarling within the passage; the bolts were not withdrawn.

"It is the gentleman, it is the strange gentleman," called the girl.

Then came again the furious shouting snarls, and the landlord's mad voice:

"Stop out, stop out there. The door won't be opened again."

"The strange gentleman is here," repeated the girl.

Then more movement was heard, and the door was suddenly opened, and the landlord rushed out upon us, wielding a broom. It was a strange sight, in the half-lighted passage. I stared blankly in the doorway. The landlord dropped the broom he was waving and collapsed as if by magic, looking at me, though he continued to mutter madly, unintelligibly.

The girl slipped past me, and the landlord snarled. Then he picked up the brush, at the same time crying:

"You are late, the door was shut, it will not be opened. We shall have the police in the house. We said twelve o'clock; at twelve o'clock the door must be shut, and must not be opened again. If you are late you stay out – "

So he went snarling, his voice rising higher and higher, away into the kitchen.

"You are coming to your room?" the landlady said to me coldly. And she led me upstairs.

The room was over the road, clean, but rather ugly, with a large tin, that had once contained lard or Swiss-milk, to wash in. But the bed was good enough, which was all that mattered.

I heard the landlord yelling, and there was a long and systematic thumping somewhere, thump, thump, thump, and banging. I wondered where it was. I could not locate it at all, because my room lay beyond another large room: I had to go through a large room, by the foot of two beds, to get to my door; so I could not quite tell where anything was.

But I went to sleep whilst I was wondering.

I woke in the morning and washed in the tin. I could see a few people in the street, walking in the Sunday morning leisure. It felt like Sunday in England, and I shrank from it. I could see none of the Italians. The factory stood there, raw and large and sombre, by the stream, and the drab-coloured stone tenements were close by. Otherwise the village was a straggling Swiss street, almost untouched.

The landlord was quiet and reasonable, even friendly, in the morning. He wanted to talk to me: where had I bought my boots, was his first question. I told him in Munich. And how much had they cost? I told him twenty-eight marks. He was much impressed by them: such good boots, of such soft, strong, beautiful leather; he had not seen such boots for a long time.

Then I knew it was he who had cleaned my boots. I could see him fingering them and wondering over them. I rather liked him. I could see he had had imagination once, and a certain fineness of nature. Now he was corrupted with drink, too far gone to be even a human being. I hated the village.

They sct bread and butter and a piece of cheese weighing about five pounds, and large, fresh, sweet cakes for breakfast. I ate and was thankful: the food was good.

A couple of village youths came in, in their Sunday clothes. They had the Sunday stiffness. It reminded me of the stiffness and curious self-consciousness that comes over life in England on a Sunday. But the landlord sat with his waistcoat hanging open over his shirt, pot-bellied, his ruined face leaning forward, talking, always talking, wanting to know.

So in a few minutes I was out on the road again, thanking God for the blessing of a road that belongs to no man, and travels away from all men.

I did not want to see the Italians. Something had got tied up in me, and I could not bear to see them again. I liked them so much; but, for some reason or other, my mind stopped like clockwork if I wanted to think of them and of what their lives would be, their future. It was as if some curious negative magnetism arrested my mind, prevented it from working, the moment I turned it towards these Italians.

I do not know why it was. But I could never write to them, or think of them, or even read the paper they gave me, though it lay in my drawer for months, in Italy, and I often glanced over six lines of it. And often, often my mind went back to the group, the play they were rehearsing, the wine in the pleasant café, and the night. But the moment my memory touched them, my whole soul stopped and was null; I could not go on. Even now I cannot really consider them in thought. I shrink involuntarily away. I do not know why this is.

THE RETURN
JOURNEY

W HEN ONE WALKS, ONE MUST TRAVEL WEST OR south. If one turns northward or eastward it is like walking down a *cul-de-sac*, to the blind end. So it has been since the Crusaders came home satiated, and the Renaissance saw the western sky as an archway into the future. So it is still. We must go westwards and southwards.

It is a sad and gloomy thing to travel even from Italy into France. But it is a joyful thing to walk south to Italy, south and west. It is so. And there is a certain exaltation in the thought of going west, even to Cornwall, to Ireland. It is as if the magnetic poles were south-west and north-east, for our spirits, with the south-west, under the sunset, as the positive pole. So whilst I walk through Switzerland, though it is a valley of gloom and depression, a light seems to flash out under every footstep, with the joy of progression.

It was Sunday morning when I left the valley where the Italians lived. I went quickly over the stream, heading for Lucerne. It was a good thing to be out of doors, with one's pack on one's back, climbing uphill. But the trees were thick by the roadside; I was not yet free. It was Sunday morning, very still.

In two hours I was at the top of the hill, looking out over the intervening valley at the long lake of Zurich, spread there beyond with its girdle of low hills, like a relief-map. I could not bear to look at it, it was so small and unreal. I had a feeling as if it were false, a large relief-map that I was looking down upon, and which I wanted to smash. It seemed to intervene between me and some reality. I could not believe that that was the real world. It was a figment, a fabrication, like a dull landscape painted on a wall, to hide the real landscape.

So I went on, over to the other side of the hill, and I looked out again. Again there were the smoky-looking hills and the lake like a piece of looking-glass. But the hills were higher: that big one was the Rigi. I set off down the hill.

There was fat agricultural land and several villages. And church was over. The church-goers were all coming home: men in black broadcloth and old chimney-pot silk hats, carrying their umbrellas; women in ugly dresses, carrying books and umbrellas. The streets were dotted with these black-clothed men and stiff women, all reduced to a Sunday nullity. I hated it. It reminded me of that which I knew in my boyhood, that stiff, null "propriety" which used to come over us, like a sort of deliberate and self-inflicted cramp, on Sundays. I hated these elders in black broadcloth, with their neutral faces, going home piously to their Sunday dinners. I hated the feeling of these villages, comfortable, well-to-do, clean, and proper.

And my boot was chafing two of my toes. That always happens. I had come down to a wide, shallow valley-bed, marshy. So about a mile out of the village I sat down by a stone bridge, by a stream, and tore up my handkerchief, and bound up the toes. And as I sat binding my toes, two of the

elders in black, with umbrellas under their arms, approached from the direction of the village.

They made me so furious, I had to hasten to fasten my boot, to hurry on again, before they should come near me. I could not bear the way they walked and talked, so crambling and material and mealy-mouthed.

Then it did actually begin to rain. I was just going down a short hill. So I sat under a bush and watched the trees drip. I was so glad to be there, homeless, without place or belonging, crouching under the leaves in the copse by the road, that I felt I had, like the meek, inherited the earth. Some men went by, with their coat-collars turned up, and the rain making still blacker their black broadcloth shoulders. They did not see me. I was as safe and separate as a ghost. So I ate the remains of my food that I had bought in Zurich, and waited for the rain.

Later, in the wet Sunday afternoon, I went on to the little lake, past many inert, neutral, material people, down an ugly road where trams ran. The blight of Sunday was almost intolerable near the town.

So on I went, by the side of the steamy, reedy lake, walking the length of it. Then suddenly I went in to a little villa by the water for tea. In Switzerland every house is a villa.

But this villa was kept by two old ladies and a delicate dog, who must not get his feet wet. I was very happy there. I had good jam and strange honey-cakes for tea, that I liked, and the little old ladies pattered round in a great stir, always whirling like two dry leaves after the restless dog.

"Why must he not go out?" I said.

"Because it is wet," they answered, "and he coughs and sneezes."

"Without a handkerchief, that is not *angenehm*," I said.

So we became bosom friends.

"You are Austrian?" they said to me.

I said I was from Graz; that my father was a doctor in Graz,

136

and that I was walking for my pleasure through the countries of Europe.

I said this because I knew a doctor from Graz who was always wandering about, and because I did not want to be myself, an Englishman, to these two old ladies. I wanted to be something else. So we exchanged confidences.

They told me, in their queer, old, toothless fashion, about their visitors, a man who used to fish all day, every day for three weeks, fish every hour of the day, though many a day he caught nothing – nothing at all – still he fished from the boat; and so on, such trivialities. Then they told me of a third sister who had died, a third little old lady. One could feel the gap in the house. They cried; and I, being an Austrian from Graz, to my astonishment felt my tears slip over on to the table. I also *was* sorry, and I would have kissed the little old ladies to comfort them.

"Only in heaven it is warm, and it doesn't rain, and no one dies," I said, looking at the wet leaves.

Then I went away. I would have stayed the night at this house: I wanted to. But I had developed my Austrian character too far.

So I went on to a detestable brutal inn in the town. And the next day I climbed over the back of the detestable Rigi, with its vile hotel, to come to Lucerne. There, on the Rigi, I met a lost young Frenchman who could speak no German, and who said he could not find people to speak French. So we sat on a stone and became close friends, and I promised faithfully to go and visit him in his barracks in Algiers: I was to sail from Naples to Algiers. He wrote me the address on his card, and told me he had friends in the regiment, to whom I should be introduced, and we could have a good time, if I would stay a week or two, down there in Algiers.

How much more real Algiers was than the rock on the Rigi where we sat, or the lake beneath, or the mountains beyond. Algiers is very real, though I have never seen it, and my friend is my friend for ever, though I have lost his card and forgotten his name. He was a Government clerk from Lyons, making this his first foreign tour before he began his military service. He showed me his "circular excursion ticket". Then at last we parted, for he must get to the top of the Rigi, and I must get to the bottom.

Lucerne and its lake were as irritating as ever – like the wrapper round milk chocolate. I could not sleep even one night there: I took the steamer down the lake, to the very last station. There I found a good German inn, and was happy.

There was a tall thin young man, whose face was red and inflamed from the sun. I thought he was a German tourist. He had just come in; and he was eating bread and milk. He and I were alone in the eating-room. He was looking at an illustrated paper.

"Does the steamer stop here all night?" I asked him in German, hearing the boat bustling and blowing her steam on the water outside, and glancing round at her lights, red and white, in the pitch darkness.

He only shook his head over his bread and milk, and did not lift his face.

"Are you English, then?" I said.

No one but an Englishman would have hidden his face in a bowl of milk, and have shaken his red ears in such painful confusion.

"Yes," he said, "I am."

And I started almost out of my skin at the unexpected London accent. It was as if one suddenly found oneself in the Tube.

"So am I," I said. "Where have you come from?"

Then he began, like a general explaining his plans, to tell me. He had walked round over the Furka Pass, had been on foot four or five days. He had walked tremendously. Knowing no German, and nothing of the mountains, he had set off alone on this tour: he had a fortnight's holiday. So he had come over the Rhone Glacier across the Furka and down from Andermatt to the Lake. On this last day he had walked about thirty mountain miles.

"But weren't you tired?" I said aghast.

He was. Under the inflamed redness of his sun- and wind- and snow-burned face he was sick with fatigue. He had done over a hundred miles in the last four days.

"Did you enjoy it?" I asked

"Oh yes. I wanted to do it all." He wanted to do it, and he *had* done it. But God knows what he wanted to do it for. He had now one day at Lucerne, one day at Interlaken and Berne, then London.

I was sorry for him in my soul, he was so cruelly tired, so perishingly victorious.

"Why did you do so much?" I said. "Why did you come on foot all down the valley when you could have taken the train? Was it worth it?"

"I think so," he said.

Yet he was sick with fatigue and over-exhaustion. His eyes were quite dark, sightless: he seemed to have lost the power of seeing, to be virtually blind. He hung his head forward when he had to write a post card, as if he felt his way. But he turned his post card so that I should not see to whom it was addressed; not that I was interested; only I noticed his little, cautious, English movement of privacy.

"What time will you be going on?" I asked.

"When is the first steamer?" he said, and he turned out a guide-book with a time-table. He would leave at about seven.

"But why so early?" I said to him.

He must be in Lucerne at a certain hour, and at Interlaken in the evening.

"I suppose you will rest when you get to London?" I said.

He looked at me quickly, reservedly.

I was drinking beer: I asked him wouldn't he have something. He thought a moment, then said he would have another glass of hot milk. The landlord came – "And bread?" he asked.

The Englishman refused. He could not eat, really. Also he was poor; he had to husband his money. The landlord brought the milk and asked me, when would the gentleman

want to go away. So I made arrangements between the land-lord and the stranger. But the Englishman was slightly un-comfortable at my intervention. He did not like me to know what he would have for breakfast.

I could feel so well the machine that had him in its grip. He slaved for a year, mechanically, in London, riding in the Tube, working in the office. Then for a fortnight he was let free. So he rushed to Switzerland, with a tour planned out, and with just enough money to see him through, and to buy presents at Interlaken: bits of the edelweiss pottery: I could see him going home with them.

So he arrived, and with amazing, pathetic courage set forth on foot in a strange land, to face strange landlords, with no language but English at his command, and his purse defi-nitely limited. Yet he wanted to go among the mountains, to cross a glacier. So he had walked on and on, like one pos-sessed, ever forward. His name might have been Excelsior, indeed.

But then, when he reached his Furka, only to walk along the ridge and to descend on the same side! My God, it was killing to the soul. And here he was, down again from the mountains, beginning his journey home again: steamer and train and steamer and train and Tube, till he was back in the machine.

It hadn't let him go, and he knew it. Hence his cruel self-torture of fatigue, his cruel exercise of courage. He who hung his head in his milk in torment when I asked him a question in German, what courage had he not needed to take this his very first trip out of England, alone, on foot!

His eyes were dark and deep with unfathomable courage. Yet he was going back in the morning. He was going back. All he had courage for was to go back. He would go back, though he died by inches. Why not? It was killing him, it was like living loaded with irons. But he had the courage to submit, to die that way, since it was the way allotted to him.

The way he sank on the table in exhaustion, drinking his milk, his will, nevertheless, so perfect and unblemished, triumphant, though his body was broken and in anguish, was almost too much to bear. My heart was wrung for my countryman, wrung till it bled.

I could not bear to understand my countryman, a man who worked for his living, as I had worked, as nearly all my countrymen work. He would not give in. On his holiday he would walk, to fulfil his purpose, walk on; no matter how cruel the effort were, he would not rest, he would not relinquish his purpose nor abate his will, not by one jot or tittle. His body must pay whatever his will demanded, though it were torture.

It all seemed to me so foolish. I was almost in tears. He went to bed. I walked by the dark lake, and talked to the girl in the inn. She was a pleasant girl: it was a pleasant inn, a homely place. One could be happy there.

In the morning it was sunny, the lake was blue. By night I should be nearly at the crest of my journey. I was glad.

The Englishman had gone. I looked for his name in the book. It was written in a fair, clerkly hand. He lived at Streatham. Suddenly I hated him. The dogged fool, to keep his nose on the grindstone like that. What was all his courage but the very tip-top cowardice? What a vile nature – almost Sadish, proud, like the infamous Red Indians, of being able to stand torture.

The landlord came to talk to me. He was fat and comfort-able and too respectful. But I had to tell him all the English-man had done, in the way of a holiday, just to shame his own fat, ponderous, inn-keeper's luxuriousness that was too gross. Then all I got out of his enormous comfortableness was:

"Yes, that's a *very* long step to take."

So I set off myself, up the valley between the close, snow-topped mountains, whose white gleamed above me as I crawled, small as an insect, along the dark, cold valley below.

There had been a cattle fair earlier in the morning, so troops of cattle were roving down the road, some with bells tang-tanging, all with soft faces and startled eyes and a sudden swerving of horns. The grass was very green by the roads and by the streams; the shadows of the mountain slopes were very dark on either hand overhead, and the sky with snowy flanks and tips was high up.

Here, away from the world, the villages were quiet and obscure – left behind. They had the same fascinating atmos-phere of being forgotten, left out of the world, that old English villages have. And buying apples and cheese and bread in a little shop that sold everything and smelled of everything, I felt at home again.

But climbing gradually higher, mile after mile, always be-tween the shadows of the high mountains, I was glad I did not live in the Alps. The villages on the slopes, the people there, seemed as if they *must* gradually, bit by bit, slide down and tumble to the water-course, and be rolled on away, away to the sea. Straggling, haphazard little villages ledged on the slope, high up, beside their wet, green, hanging meadows, with pine trees behind and the valley bottom far below, and rocks right above, on both sides, seemed like little temporary squattings of outcast people. It seemed impossible that they should persist there, with great shadows wielded over them, like a menace, and gleams of brief sunshine, like a window. There was a sense of momentariness and expectation. It seemed as though some dramatic upheaval must take place, the mountains fall down into their own shadows. The valley beds were like deep graves, the sides of the mountains like the collapsing walls of a grave. The very mountain-tops above, bright with transcendent snow, seemed like death, eternal death.

There, it seemed, in the glamorous snow, was the source of death, which fell down in great waves of shadow and rock, rushing to the level earth. And all the people of the mountains, on the slopes, in the valleys, seemed to live upon this great, rushing wave of death, of breaking-down, of destruction.

The very pure source of breaking-down, decomposition, the very quick of cold death, is the snowy mountain-peak above. There, eternally, goes on the white foregathering of the crystals, out of the deathly cold of the heavens; this is the static nucleus where death meets life in its elementality. And thence, from their white, radiant nucleus of death in life, flows the great flux downwards, towards life and warmth.

And we below, we cannot think of the flux upwards, that flows from the needle-point of snow to the unutterable cold and death.

The people under the mountains, they seem to live in the flux of death, the last, strange, overshadowed units of life. Big shadows wave over them, there is the eternal noise of water falling icily downwards from the source of death overhead.

And the people under the shadows, dwelling in the tang of snow and the noise of icy water, seem dark, almost sordid, brutal. There is no flowering or coming to flower, only this persistence, in the ice-touched air, of reproductive life.

But it is difficult to get a sense of a native population. Everywhere are the hotels and the foreigners, the parasitism. Yet there is, unseen, this overshadowed, overhung, sordid mountain population, ledged on the slopes and in the crevices. In the wider valleys there is still a sense of cowering among the people. But they catch a new tone from their contact with the foreigners. And in the towns are nothing but tradespeople.

So I climbed slowly up, for a whole day, first along the high-road, sometimes above and sometimes below the twisting, serpentine railway, then afterwards along a path on the side of the hill – a path that went through the crew-yards of isolated farms and even through the garden of a village priest. The priest was decorating an archway. He stood on a chair in the sunshine, reaching up with a garland, whilst the serving-woman stood below, talking loudly.

The valley here seemed wider, the great flanks of the mountains gave place, the peaks above were further back. So one was happier. I was pleased as I sat by the thin track of single flat stones that dropped swiftly downhill.

At the bottom was a little town with a factory or quarry, or a foundry, some place with long, smoking chimneys; which made me feel quite at home among the mountains.

It is the hideous rawness of the world of men, the horrible, desolating harshness of the advance of the industrial world upon the world of nature, that is so painful. It looks as though the industrial spread of mankind were a sort of dry disintegration advancing and advancing, a process of dry disintegration. If only we could learn to take thought for the whole world instead of for merely tiny bits of it.

I went through the little, hideous, crude factory-settlement in the high valley, where the eternal snows gleamed, past the enormous advertisements for chocolate and hotels, up the last steep slope of the pass to where the tunnel begins. Göschenen, the village at the mouth of the tunnel, is all railway sidings and haphazard villas for tourists, post cards, and touts and weedy carriages; disorder and sterile chaos, high up. How should any one stay there!

I went on up the pass itself. There were various parties of visitors on the roads and tracks, people from towns incongruously walking and driving. It was drawing on to evening. I climbed slowly, between the great cleft in the rock where are the big iron gates, through which the road winds, winds half-way down the narrow gulley of solid, living rock, the very throat of the path, where hangs a tablet in memory of many Russians killed.

Emerging through the dark rocky throat of the pass I came to the upper world, the level upper world. It was evening, livid, cold. On either side spread the sort of moorland of the wide pass-head. I drew near along the high-road, to Andermatt.

Everywhere were soldiers moving about the livid, desolate waste of this upper world. I passed the barracks and the first villas for visitors. Darkness was coming on; the straggling, inconclusive street of Andermatt looked as if it were some accident – houses, hotels, barracks, lodging-places tumbled at random as the caravan of civilisation crossed this high, cold, arid bridge of the European world.

I bought two post cards and wrote them out of doors in the cold, livid twilight. Then I asked a soldier where was the post-office. He directed me. It was something like sending post cards from Skegness or Bognor, there in the post-office.

I was trying to make myself agree to stay in Andermatt for the night. But I could not. The whole place was so terribly raw and flat and accidental, as if great pieces of furniture had tumbled out of a pantechnicon and lay discarded by the road. I hovered in the street, in the twilight, trying to make myself stay. I looked at the announcements of lodgings and boarding for visitors. It was no good. I could not go into one of these houses.

So I passed on, through the old, low, broad-eaved houses that cringe down to the very street, out into the open again. The air was fierce and savage. On one side was a moorland, level; on the other a sweep of naked hill, curved concave, and sprinkled with snow. I could see how wonderful it would all be, under five or six feet of winter snow, ski-ing and tobogganing at Christmas. But it needed the snow. In the summer there is to be seen nothing but the winter's broken detritus.

The twilight deepened, though there was still the strange, glassy translucency of the snow-lit air. A fragment of moon was in the sky. A carriage-load of French tourists passed me. There was the loud noise of water, as ever, something eternal and maddening in its sound, like the sound of Time itself, rustling and rushing and wavering, but never for a second ceasing. The rushing of Time that continues throughout eternity, this is the sound of the icy streams of Switzerland, something that mocks and destroys our warm being.

So I came, in the early darkness, to the little village with the broken castle that stands for ever frozen at the point where the track parts, one way continuing along the ridge to the Furka Pass, the other swerving over the hill to the left, over the Gotthardt.

In this village I must stay. I saw a woman looking hastily, furtively from a doorway. I knew she was looking for visitors. I went on up the hilly street. There were only a few wooden houses and a gaily lighted wooden inn, where men were laughing, and strangers, men, standing talking loudly in the doorway.

It was very difficult to go to a house this night. I did not want to approach any of them. I turned back to the house of the peering woman. She had looked hen-like and anxious. She would be glad of a visitor to help her pay her rent.

It was a clean, pleasant wooden house, made to keep out the cold. That seemed its one function: to defend the inmates from the cold. It was furnished like a hut, just tables and chairs and bare wooden walls. One felt very close and secure in the room, as in a hut, shut away from the outer world.

The hen-like woman came.

"Can I have a bed," I said, "for the night?"

"Abendessen, ja!" she replied. "Will you have soup and boiled beef and vegetables?"

I said I would, so I sat down to wait, in the utter silence. I could scarcely hear the ice-stream, the silence seemed frozen, the house empty. The woman seemed to be flitting aimlessly, scurriedly, in reflex against the silence. One could almost touch the stillness as one could touch the walls, or the stove, or the table with white American oil-cloth.

Suddenly she appeared again.

"What will you drink?"

She watched my face anxiously, and her voice was pathetic, slightly pleading in its quickness.

"Wine or beer?" she said.

I would not trust the coldness of beer.

"A half of red wine," I said.

I knew she was going to keep me an indefinite time.

She appeared with the wine and bread.

"Would you like omelette after the beef?" she asked. "Omelette with cognac – I can make it *very* good."

I knew I should be spending too much, but I said yes. After all, why should I not eat, after the long walk?

So she left me again, whilst I sat in the utter isolation and stillness, eating bread and drinking the wine, which was good. And I listened for any sound: only the faint noise of the stream. And I wondered, Why am I here, on this ridge of the Alps, in the lamp-lit, wooden, close-shut room, alone? Why am I here?

Yet somehow I was glad, I was happy even: such splendid silence and coldness and clean isolation. It was something eternal, unbroachable: I was free, in this heavy, ice-cold air, this upper world, alone. London, far away below, beyond, England, Germany, France – they were all so unreal in the night. It was a sort of grief that this continent all beneath was so unreal, false, non-existent in its activity. Out of the silence one looked down on it, and it seemed to have lost all importance, all significance. It was so big, yet it had no significance. The kingdoms of the world had no significance: what could one do but wander about.

The woman came with my soup. I asked her, did not many people come in the summer. But she was scared away, she did not answer, she went like a leaf in the wind. However, the soup was good and plentiful.

She was a long time before she came with the next course. Then she put the tray on the table, and looking at me, then looking away, shrinking, she said:

"You must excuse me if I don't answer you – I don't hear well – I am rather deaf."

I looked at her, and I winced also. She shrank in such simple pain from the fact of her defect. I wondered if she were bullied because of it, or only afraid lest visitors would dislike it.

She put the dishes in order, set me my plate, quickly, nervously, and was gone again, like a scared chicken. Being tired, I wanted to weep over her, the nervous, timid hen, so frightened by her own deafness. The house was silent of her, empty. It was perhaps her deafness which created this empty soundlessness.

When she came with the omelette, I said to her loudly:

"That was very good, the soup and meat." She quivered nervously, and said, "Thank you," and I managed to talk to her. She was like most deaf people, in that her terror of not hearing made her six times worse than she actually was.

She spoke with a soft, strange accent, so I thought she was perhaps a foreigner. But when I asked her she misunderstood, and I had not the heart to correct her. I can only remember she said her house was always full in the winter, about Christmas-time. People came for the winter sport. There were two young English ladies who always came to her.

She spoke of them warmly. Then, suddenly afraid, she drifted off again. I ate the omelette with cognac, which was very good, then I looked in the street. It was very dark, with bright stars, and smelled of snow. Two village men went by. I was tired, I did not want to go to the inn.

So I went to bed, in the silent, wooden house. I had a small bedroom, clean and wooden and very cold. Outside, the stream was rushing. I covered myself with a great depth of feather-bed, and looked at the stars, and the shadowy upper world, and went to sleep.

In the morning I washed in the ice-cold water, and was glad to set out. An icy mist was over the noisy stream, there were a few meagre, shredded pine trees. I had breakfast and paid my bill: it was seven francs – more than I could afford; but that did not matter, once I was out in the air.

The sky was blue and perfect, it was a ringing morning, the village was very still. I went up the hill till I came to the sign-post. I looked down the direction of the Furka, and thought of my tired Englishman from Streatham, who would be on his way home. Thank God I need not go home: never, perhaps. I turned up the track to the left, to the Gothard.

Standing looking round at the mountain-tops, at the village and the broken castle below me, at the scattered débris of Andermatt on the moor in the distance, I was jumping in my soul with delight. Should one ever go down to the lower world?

Then I saw another figure striding along, a youth with knee-breeches and Alpine hat and braces over his shirt, walking manfully, his coat slung in his Rucksack behind. I laughed, and waited. He came my way.

"Are you going over the Gothard?" I said.

"Yes," he replied. "Are you also?"

"Yes," I said. "We will go together."

So we set off, climbing a track up the heathy rocks.

He was a pale, freckled town youth from Basel, seventeen years old. He was a clerk in a baggage-transport firm –

Gondrand Frères, I believe. He had a week's holiday, in which time he was going to make a big circular walk, something like the Englishman's. But he was accustomed to this mountain walking: he belonged to a Sportverein. Manfully he marched in his thick hob-nailed boots, earnestly he scrambled up the rocks.

We were in the crest of the pass. Broad snow-patched slopes came down from the pure sky; the defile was full of stones, all bare stones, enormous ones as big as a house, and small ones, pebbles. Through these the road wound in silence, through this upper, transcendent desolation, wherein was only the sound of the stream. Sky and snow-patched slopes, then the stony, rocky bed of the defile, full of morning sunshine: this was all. We were crossing in silence from the northern world to the southern.

But he, Emil, was going to take the train back, through the tunnel, in the evening, to resume his circular walk at Göschenen.

I, however, was going on, over the ridge of the world, from the north into the south. So I was glad.

We climbed up the gradual incline for a long time. The slopes above became lower, they began to recede. The sky was very near, we were walking under the sky.

Then the defile widened out, there was an open place before us, the very top of the pass. Also there were low barracks, and soldiers. We heard firing. Standing still, we saw on the slopes of snow, under the radiant blue heaven, tiny puffs of smoke, then some small black figures crossing the snow patch, then another rattle of rifle-fire, rattling dry and unnatural in the upper, skyey air, between the rocks.

"Das ist schön," said my companion, in his simple admiration.

"Hübsch," I said.

"But that would be splendid, to be firing up there, manoeuvring up in the snow."

And he began to tell me how hard a soldier's life was, how hard the soldier was drilled.

"You don't look forward to it?" I said.

"Oh yes, I do. I want to be a solider, I want to serve my time."

"Why?" I said.

"For the exercise, the life, the drilling. One becomes strong."

"Do all the Swiss want to serve their time in the army?" I asked.

"Yes – they all want to. It is good for every man, and it keeps us all together. Besides, it is only for a year. For a year it is very good. The Germans have three years – that is too long, and that is bad."

I told him how the soldiers in Bavaria hated the military service.

"Yes," he said, "that is true of Germans. The system is different. Ours is much better; in Switzerland a man enjoys his time as a soldier. I want to go."

So we watched the black dots of soldiers crawling over the high snow, listened to the unnatural dry rattle of guns, up there.

Then we were aware of somebody whistling, of soldiers yelling down the road. We were to come on, along the level, over the bridge. So we marched quickly forward, away from the slopes, towards the hotel, once a monastery, that stood in the distance. The light was blue and clear on the reedy lakes of this upper place; it was a strange desolation of water and bog and rocks and road, hedged by the snowy slopes round the rim, under the very sky.

The soldier was yelling again. I could not tell what he said.

"He says if we don't run we can't come at all." said Emil.

"I won't run," I said.

So we hurried forwards, over the bridge, where the soldier on guard was standing.

"Do you want to be shot?" he said angrily, as we came up.

"No thanks," I said.

Emil was very serious.

"How long should we have had to wait if we hadn't got through now?" he asked the soldier, when we were safely out of danger.

"Till one o'clock," was the reply.

"Two hours!" said Emil, strangely elated. "We should have had to wait two hours before we could come on. He was riled that we didn't run," and he laughed with glee.

So we marched over the level to the hotel. We called in for a glass of hot milk. I asked in German. But the maid, a pert hussy, elegant and superior, was French. She served us with great contempt, as two worthless creatures, poverty-stricken. It abashed poor Emil, but we managed to laugh at her. This made her very angry. In the smoking-room she raised up her voice in French:

"Du lait chaud pour les chameaux."

"Some hot milk for the camels, she says," I translated for Emil. He was covered with confusion and youthful anger.

But I called to her, tapped the table and called:

"Mademoiselle!"

She appeared flouncingly in the doorway.

"Encore du lait pour les chameaux," I said.

And she whisked our glasses off the table, and flounced out without a word.

But she would not come in again with the milk. A German girl brought it. We laughed, and she smiled primly.

When we set forth again, Emil rolled up his sleeves and turned back his shirt from his neck and breast, to do the thing thoroughly. Besides, it was midday, and the sun was hot; and, with his bulky pack on his back, he suggested the camel of the French maid more than ever.

We were on the downward slope. Only a short way from the hotel, and there was the drop, the great cleft in the mountains running down from this shallow pot among the peaks.

The descent on the south side is much more precipitous and wonderful than the ascent from the north. On the south, the rocks are craggy and stupendous; the little river falls head-long down; it is not a stream, it is one broken, panting cascade far away in the gulley below, in the darkness.

But on the slopes the sun pours in, the road winds down with its tail in its mouth, always in endless loops returning on itself. The mules that travel upward seem to be treading in a mill.

Emil took the narrow tracks, and, like the water, we cascaded down, leaping from level to level, leaping, running, leaping, descending headlong, only resting now and again when we came down on to another level of the high-road.

Having begun, we could not help ourselves, we were like two stones bouncing down. Emil was highly elated. He waved his thin, bare, white arms as he leapt, his chest grew pink with the exercise. Now he felt he was doing something that became a member of his Sportverein. Down we went, jumping, running, britching.

It was wonderful on this south side, so sunny, with feathery trees and deep black shadows. It reminded me of Goethe, of the romantic period:

Kennst du das Land, wo die Citronen blühen?

So we went tumbling down into the south, very swiftly, along with the tumbling stream. But it was very tiring. We went at a great pace down the gully, between the sheer rocks. Trees grew in the ledges high over our heads, trees grew down below. And ever we descended.

Till gradually the gully opened, then opened into a wide valley-head, and we saw Airolo away below us, the railway emerging from its hole, the whole valley like a cornucopia full of sunshine.

Poor Emil was tired, more tired than I was. And his big boots had hurt his feet in the descent. So, having come to the

open valley-head, we went more gently. He had become rather quiet.

The head of the valley had that half-tamed, ancient aspect that reminded me of the Romans. I could only expect the Roman legions to be encamped down there; and the white goats feeding on the bushes belonged to a Roman camp.

But no, we saw again the barracks of the Swiss soldiery, and again we were in the midst of rifle-fire and manoeuvres. But we went evenly, tired now, and hungry. We had nothing to eat.

It is strange how different the sun-dried, ancient, southern slopes of the world are, from the northern slopes. It is as if the god Pan really had his home among these sun-bleached stones and tough, sun-dark trees. And one knows it all in one's blood, it is pure, sun-dried memory. So I was content, coming down into Airolo.

We found the streets were Italian, the houses sunny outside and dark within, like Italy, there were laurels in the road. Poor Emil was a foreigner all at once. He rolled down his shirt sleeves and fastened his shirt-neck, put on his coat and collar, and became a foreigner in his soul, pale and strange.

I saw a shop with vegetables and grapes, a real Italian shop, a dark cave.

"Quanto costa l' uva?" were my first words in the south.

"Sessanta al chilo," said the girl.

And it was as pleasant as a drink of wine, the Italian.

So Emil and I ate the sweet black grapes as we went to the station.

He was very poor. We went into the third-class restaurant at the station. He ordered beer and bread and sausage; I ordered soup and boiled beef and vegetables.

They brought me a great quantity, so, whilst the girl was serving coffee-with-rum to the men at the bar, I took another spoon and knife and fork and plates for Emil, and we had two dinners from my one. When the girl – she was a woman of thirty-five – came back, she looked at us sharply. I smiled at her coaxingly; so she gave a small, kindly smile in reply.

"Ja, dies ist reizend," said Eil, *sotto voce*, exulting. He was very shy. But we were curiously happy, in that railway restaurant.

Then we sat very still, on the platform, and waited for the train. It was like Italy, pleasant and social to wait in the railway station, all the world easy and warm in its activity, with the sun shining.

I decided to take a franc's worth of train-journey. So I chose my station. It was one franc twenty, third class. Then my train came, and Emil and I parted, he waving to me till I was out of sight. I was sorry he had to go back, he did so want to venture forth.

So I slid for a dozen miles or more, sleepily, down the Ticino valley, sitting opposite two fat priests in their feminine black.

When I got out at my station I felt for the first time ill at ease. Why was I getting out at this wayside place, on to the great, raw high-road? I did not know. But I set off walking. It was nearly tea-time.

Nothing in the world is more ghastly than these Italian roads, new, mechanical, belonging to a machine life. The old roads are wonderful, skilfully aiming their way. But these new great roads are desolating, more desolating than all the ruins in the world.

I walked on and on, down the Ticino valley, towards Bellinzona. The valley was perhaps beautiful: I don't know. I can only remember the road. It was broad and new, and it ran very often beside the railway. It ran also by quarries and by occasional factories, also through villages. And the quality of its sordidness is something that does not bear thinking of, a quality that has entered Italian life now, if it was not there before.

Here and there, where there were quarries or industries, great lodging-houses stood naked by the road, great, grey, desolate places; and squalid children were playing round the steps, and dirty men slouched in. Everything seemed under a weight.

Down the road of the Ticino valley I felt again my terror of this new world which is coming into being on top of us. One always feels it in a suburb, on the edge of a town, where the land is being broken under the advance of houses. But this is nothing, in England, to the terror one feels on the new Italian roads, where these great blind cubes of dwellings rise stark from the destroyed earth, swarming with a sort of verminous life, really verminous, purely destructive.

It seems to happen when the peasant suddenly leaves his home and becomes a workman. Then an entire change comes over everywhere. Life is now a matter of selling oneself to slave-work, building roads or labouring in quarries or mines or on the railways, purposeless, meaningless, really slave-work, each integer doing his mere labour, and all for no purpose, except to have money, and to get away from the old system.

These Italian navvies work all day long, their whole life is engaged in the mere brute labour. And they are the navvies of the world. And whilst they are navvying, they are almost shockingly indifferent to their circumstances, merely callous to the dirt and foulness.

It is as if the whole social form were breaking down, and the human element swarmed within the disintegration, like maggots in cheese. The roads, the railways are built, the mines and quarries are excavated, but the whole organism of life, the social organism, is slowly crumbling and caving in, in a kind of process of dry rot, most terrifying to see. So that it seems as though we should be left at last with a great system of roads and railways and industries, and a world of utter chaos seething upon these fabrications: as if we had created a steel framework, and the whole body of society were crumbling and rotting in between. It is most terrifying to realise; and I have always felt this terror upon a new Italian high-road – more there than anywhere.

The remembrance of the Ticino valley is a sort of nightmare to me. But it was better when at last, in the darkness of night, I got into Bellinzona. In the midst of the town one felt the old organism still living. It is only at its extremities that it is falling to pieces, as in dry rot.

In the morning, leaving Bellinzona, again I went in terror of the new, evil high-road, with its skirting of huge cubical houses and its seething navvy population. Only the peasants driving in with fruit were consoling. But I was afraid of them: the same spirit had set in in them.

I was no longer happy in Switzerland, not even when I was eating great blackberries and looking down at the Lago Maggiore, at Locarno, lying by the lake; the terror of the callous, disintegrating process was too strong in me.

At a little inn a man was very good to me. He went into his garden and fetched me the first grapes and apples and peaches, bringing them in amongst leaves, and heaping them before me. He was Italian-Swiss; he had been in a bank in Bern; now he had retired, had bought his paternal home, and was a free man. He was about fifty years old; he spent all his time in his garden; his daughter attended to the inn.

He talked to me, as long as I stayed, about Italy and Switzerland and work and life. He was retired, he was free. But he was only nominally free. He had only achieved freedom from labour. He knew that the system he had escaped at last, persisted, and would consume his sons and his grandchildren. He himself had more or less escaped back to the old form; but as he came with me on to the hill-side, looking down the high-road at Lugano in the distance, he knew that his old order was collapsing by a slow process of disintegration.

Why did he talk to me as if I had any hope, as if I represented any positive truth as against this great negative truth that was advancing up the hill-side. Again I was afraid. I

hastened down the high-road, past the houses, the grey, raw crystals of corruption.

I saw a girl with handsome bare legs, ankles shining like brass in the sun. She was working in a field, on the edge of a vineyard. I stopped to look at her, suddenly fascinated by her handsome naked flesh that shone like brass.

Then she called out to me, in a jargon I could not understand, something mocking and challenging. And her voice was raucous and challenging; I went on, afraid.

In Lugano I stayed at a German hotel. I remember sitting on a seat in the darkness by the lake, watching the stream of promenaders patrolling the edge of the water, under the trees and the lamps. I can still see many of their faces: English, German, Italian, French. And it seemed here, here in this holiday-place, was the quick of the disintegration, the dry-rot, in this dry, friable flux of people backwards and forwards on the edge of the lake, men and women from the big hotels, in evening dress, curiously sinister, and ordinary visitors, and tourists, and workmen, youths, men of the town, laughing, jeering. It was curiously and painfully sinister, almost obscene.

I sat a long time among them, thinking of the girl with her limbs of glowing brass. Then at last I went up to the hotel, and sat in the lounge looking at the papers. It was the same

here as down below, though not so intense, the feeling of horror.

So I went to bed. The hotel was on the edge of a steep declivity. I wondered why the whole hills did not slide down, in some great natural catastrophe.

In the morning I walked along the side of the Lake of Lugano, to where I could take a steamer to ferry me down to the end. The lake is not beautiful, only picturesque. I liked most to think of the Romans coming to it.

So I steamed down to the lower end of the water. When I landed and went along by a sort of railway I saw a group of men. Suddenly they began to whoop and shout. They were hanging on to an immense pale bullock, which was slung up to be shod; and it was lunging and kicking with terrible energy. It was strange to see that mass of pale, soft-looking flesh working with such violent frenzy, convulsed with violent, active frenzy, whilst men and women hung on to it with ropes, hung on and weighed it down. But again it scattered some of them in its terrible convulsion. Human beings scattered into the road, the whole place was covered with hot dung. And when the bullock began to lunge again, the men set up a howl, half of triumph, half of derision.

I went on, not wanting to see. I went along a very dusty

road. But it was not so terrifying, this road. Perhaps it was older.

In a dreary little Chiasso I drank coffee, and watched the come and go through the Customs. The Swiss and the Italian Customs officials had their offices within a few yards of each other, and everybody must stop. I went in and showed my Rucksack to the Italian, then I mounted a tram, and went to the Lake of Como.

In the tram were dressed-up women, fashionable, but business-like. They had come by train to Chiasso, or else had been shopping in the town.

When we came to the terminus a young miss, dismounting before me, left behind her parasol. I had been conscious of my dusty, grimy appearance as I sat in the tram, I knew they thought me a workman on the roads. However, I forgot that when it was time to dismount.

"Pardon, Mademoiselle," I said to the young miss. She turned and withered me with a rather overdone contempt – "bourgeoise," I said to myself, as I looked at her – "Vous avez laissé votre parasol."

She turned, and with a rapacious movement darted upon her parasol. How her soul was in her possessions! I stood and watched her. Then she went into the road and under the trees, haughty, a demoiselle. She had on white kid boots.

I thought of the Lake of Como what I had thought of Lugano: it must have been wonderful when the Romans came there. Now it is all villas. I think only the sunrise is still wonderful, sometimes.

I took the steamer down to Como, and slept in a vast old stone cavern of an inn, a remarkable place, with rather nice people. In the morning I went out. The peace and the bygone beauty of the cathedral created the glow of the great past. And in the market-place they were selling chestnuts wholesale, great heaps of bright, brown chestnuts, and sacks of chestnuts, and peasants very eager selling and buying. I thought of Como, it must have been wonderful even a hundred years ago. Now it is cosmopolitan, the cathedral is like a relic, a museum object, everywhere stinks of mechanical money-pleasure.

I dared not risk walking to Milan: I took the train. And there, in Milan, sitting in the Cathedral Square, on Saturday afternoon, drinking Bitter Campari and watching the swarm of Italian city-men drink and talk vivaciously, I saw that here the life was still vivid, here the process of disintegration was vigorous, and centred in a multiplicity of mechanical activities that engage the human mind as well as the body. But always there was the same purpose stinking in it all, the mechanising, the perfect mechanising of human life.

ACKNOWLEDGEMENTS